200 Years with San-J

Featuring Recipes Using Tamari Soy Sauce

RECIPES BY ROBIN TAYLOR SWATT

Pascoe Publishing, Inc.

Rocklin, California

Cover & Interior Design by Knockout Books

Published in the United States of America by
Pascoe Publishing, Inc.
Rocklin, California
http://www.pascoepublishing.com

✻

ISBN: 1-929862-25-3

03 04 05 10 9 8 7 6 5 4 3 2 1

Printed in China

Table of Contents

Dedication

— ⋈ —

To our loyal consumers

who have made it

possible for the Sato family

to produce premium

Tamari for 200 years.

❋

In 1804, Magoemon Sato fulfilled his dream by starting a miso and Tamari company called the San Jirushi Corporation. Passed down by the Sato family from generation to generation, San Jirushi is now 200 years old and is the leading manufacturer of Tamari in Japan. In 1987, the company established San-J International and built a brewery plant in Virginia. Today San-J maintains the rich tradition of the Sato family, providing high-quality products that delight consumers throughout North America and Europe.

Introduction

We invite you to join in culinary pleasures that are 200 years in the making.

San Jirushi began as a Tamari and miso manufacturer in the year 1804. In 1978, they began to sell Tamari to the U.S. market. Different than ordinary soy sauce because of its natural flavor-enhancing properties, Tamari was well received in the States. In 1987, San Jirushi built the first and only Tamari brewing plant in the United States. The plant is located in Richmond, Virginia. With the American consumer in mind, the company name was shortened to San-J, a name that could be more easily remembered. Two hundred years later, San-J is still using the same traditional Japanese methods developed by San Jirushi to brew their premium Tamari.

As the popularity of Asian flavors has grown in the United States, San-J has responded with a full line of Asian-inspired Cooking Sauces, Salad Dressings, Rice Crackers and Soups.

To celebrate our 200 year anniversary, San-J has developed this cookbook to honor its origins in Japan and to commemorate its new roots in the United States.

Bring a bit of Eastern culture into your home by trying the authentic Japanese recipes included in this cookbook. Or add our sauces to tried and true traditional American fare. San-J sauces will give every meal a depth of flavor previously only found in restaurants.

What is Tamari

Tamari is one of Japan's oldest and best kept culinary secrets. Its roots go back to the original soy sauce, conceived in China and brought to Japan along with Buddhism in the 7th century A.D. It has been known since ancient times that cooked soybeans, exposed to certain microbiological cultures and aged in salt, will produce a tasty, dark red paste. The Japanese call this fermented soybean paste "miso." Tamari means "that which accumulates" and was the name given to the protein-rich liquid that accumulates during the miso ripening process. Tamari has become a highly prized seasoning.

Tamari can be compared to the fine wine of soy sauces. Tamari is a premium soy sauce brewed primarily with soybeans and little or no wheat resulting in a rich, complex, well-balanced seasoning. The high concentration of soybeans gives Tamari its unique properties. With Tamari, your taste buds can detect not only salt, but sweet, sour, bitter and the fifth sense - umami. Ordinary soy sauce contains 40-60% wheat and triggers mostly the salt taste buds.

Tamari is naturally brewed for up to six months. The high content of soybeans used when fermenting Tamari results in more soy protein. This soy protein, in the form of 18 amino acids, makes Tamari a versatile yet complex flavor enhancer. The presence of more proteins allows superior heat stability as demonstrated by its uniform flavor retention when heated or used in microwavable foods.

By using Tamari as a substitute for salt, sodium levels can be significantly reduced without compromising taste. Tamari is a wonderful addition to meats, poultry, seafood, vegetables, baked goods, sauces and snack foods.

We encourage you to experiment and discover the wonders of how Tamari can enhance the flavors of everything you create in your kitchen.

Gyoza (PORK POTSTICKERS)

This recipe can be adapted to use any kind of meat—ground turkey, ground beef or flaked crabmeat.
Potstickers can be used naturally and easily as excellent appetizers, however they can also
become a casual main course. They're always delicious.

Ingredients for Pork Potstickers

1 1/2 pounds	ground pork
1 head	green cabbage, very finely chopped
4 cloves	garlic, minced
1 tablespoon	fresh ginger, finely minced
1 small	yellow onion, peeled and minced
6	fresh or reconstituted shiitake mushrooms, stems removed, finely diced
1 teaspoon	toasted sesame oil
1 tablespoon	San-J Tamari
1 small	egg, beaten (optional)
2 packages	round potsticker wrappers
	small bowl of warm water
	vegetable oil

San-J Tamari Dipping Sauce

2 tablespoons	San-J Tamari
1/2	lime or lemon, juiced
1/2 teaspoon	toasted sesame oil
1/2 teaspoon	dried red pepper flakes

In a medium mixing bowl, prepare the potsticker filling by combining the pork, cabbage, garlic, ginger, onion, mushrooms, sesame oil and San-J Tamari until just combined. If the mixture does not adhere, add the optional beaten egg as a binder.

To stuff the potsticker wrappers, dip your index finger into the warm water and moisten the entire outer edge of one potsticker wrapper. Scoop 1 teaspoon of the filling and place the filling in the center of the wrapper. Fold over the wrapper to create a pouch and crimp the edges shut with your fingers. Place on a baking sheet and cover with a damp dishtowel. This prevents the potstickers from becoming dry. You may sprinkle the cookie sheet with a little cornstarch to keep the potstickers from sticking to each other. Continue stuffing and crimping until you have prepared at least 80 potstickers. (Note: At this point, you may freeze any remaining filling for future use.)

In a large sauté pan, heat 2 tablespoons of vegetable oil to medium heat. Cook the potstickers in batches, 6 at a time, without crowding the pan. Brown one side of the potstickers and add 1 to 2 tablespoons of water. Quickly cover the sauté pan with an airtight lid to steam the potstickers. As soon as the water has evaporated, remove the potstickers to a warmed serving platter. Keep warm as you repeat the cooking process with the remaining potstickers.

To prepare the San-J Tamari Dipping Sauce, combine the San-J Tamari, lime or lemon juice, sesame oil and red pepper flakes in a small bowl. Whisk thoroughly and let stand for several minutes to allow the flavors to marry. Serve the potstickers with the sauce.

MAKES ABOUT 80 POTSTICKERS.

Broiled Gorgonzola & Walnut Portobello Mushrooms

Sumptuously rich wedges of nuts, cheese and earthy mushrooms.

Ingredients

4 large	portobello mushroom caps, cleaned and patted dry
2 tablespoons	extra virgin olive oil
1/4 cup	San-J Tamari
1/2 cup	walnuts, toasted and chopped
1/2 cup	gorgonzola cheese, crumbled

Brush both sides of each mushroom cap with olive oil. Drizzle the interior of each cap with the San-J Tamari. To toast the walnuts, place the chopped nuts on an ungreased baking sheet and broil for 2 to 3 minutes, turning the nuts carefully as they brown. Place the mushroom caps on a nonstick baking sheet. Preheat the broiler for 3 minutes. Place the baking sheet with the mushrooms about 4 inches under the broiler and broil for 3 minutes. Watch carefully to prevent burning. Remove the mushrooms from the broiler and sprinkle the interior of the caps evenly with the chopped walnuts and gorgonzola cheese. Position the mushrooms under the broiler again for an additional 2 minutes, or until the cheese is melted and the caps are softened. Remove and cut each mushroom into thin wedges to serve as an appetizer. You may also serve each whole cap as a meatless main dish, if desired.

MAKES 4 SERVINGS.

Eastern Tamari-Roasted Nuts

Walnuts, cashews and pecans create the perfect foundation for an exotic dusting of Eastern spices. Serve the flavored nuts with a casual white wine at your next dinner party.

Ingredients

1/4 pound	walnut halves
1/4 pound	pecan halves
1 pound	whole cashews
1/2 cup	sugar
2 tablespoons	vegetable oil
1/2 teaspoon	salt
1/4 teaspoon	ground black pepper
1 1/4 teaspoon	ground cumin
1/4 teaspoon	ground coriander
1/2 teaspoon	ground ginger
1/4 teaspoon	ground cloves
1/2 to 1 teaspoon	ground chili powder
1 tablespoon	San-J Tamari
1	lime, juiced

Preheat the oven to 325°F. Place the nuts in a large bowl and pour boiling water over the nuts to cover. Blanch the nuts for one minute and drain well in a large strainer. Place the hot nuts in a large mixing bowl and combine with the sugar and vegetable oil. Mix well and set aside for 10 minutes to rest.

Pour the nuts in a single layer onto a lightly greased baking sheet. Bake for 30 minutes, turning every 10 minutes, until the nuts are uniformly brown and crispy. Remove the nuts to a bowl and toss with the salt, pepper, cumin, coriander, ginger, cloves, chili powder, San-J Tamari and lime juice. Spread the nuts in a single layer on a baking sheet to cool. When completely cool, store in an airtight container.

SERVES APPROXIMATELY 24.

Chicken Satay with Peanut Sauce

An Asian classic, this dish combines the juiciness of chicken with the clean citrus flavors of lime and green curry. San-J's Thai Peanut Sauce is the perfect companion to these winning appetizers.

Ingredients

4	boneless, skinless chicken breasts
1/4 cup	fresh lime juice
1 teaspoon	honey
1 tablespoon	green Thai curry paste
12	wooden skewers, soaked in water for at least 30 minutes
2 tablespoons	fresh cilantro, minced
3/4 cup	San-J Thai Peanut Sauce

Cut each chicken breast into 3 long strips. In a medium mixing bowl, combine the lime juice, honey and curry paste and add the chicken breast strips to marinate. Cover and marinate in the refrigerator for at least 30 minutes or up to 2 hours. Thread each chicken strip onto a skewer vertically, weaving the chicken back and forth. Position the rack about 6 inches away from the oven broiler and preheat for 3 minutes. Place the chicken skewers on a baking sheet and broil for 3 minutes on each side, or until cooked through completely. Garnish each skewer with a sprinkling of fresh cilantro and serve with the San-J Thai Peanut Sauce for dipping.

MAKES 6 SERVINGS.

Asian BBQ Chicken Wings

Crispy chicken wings are well-dressed with San-J Asian BBQ Sauce.
This simple pairing results in an exciting introduction to any meal.

Ingredients

2 cups	San-J Asian BBQ Sauce
3 pounds	chicken wings, cleaned and small tips discarded

In a large mixing bowl, combine the San-J Asian BBQ Sauce and chicken wings. Mix thoroughly so that the wings are uniformly well-coated. Cover tightly and marinate in the refrigerator for at least 30 minutes or up to 2 hours. Remove the wings from the marinade and place the wings in a single layer on a baking sheet lined with foil. Place in a preheated 350°F oven. In a saucepan, heat the marinade to boiling and cook for 5 minutes. Turn the wings every 15 minutes while baking and baste each time, with the remaining sauce. Bake for 1 hour or until completely cooked through.

MAKES 12 SERVINGS.

Vietnamese Salad Rolls

Vietnamese salad rolls have become very popular throughout the world, probably because they are light and carry the fresh flavors of basil, mint and cilantro. You may gently warm the San-J Thai Peanut Sauce before serving for additional flavor, if desired.

Ingredients

8 ounces	fresh raw medium shrimp, deveined and tails removed
8 large	round rice paper wrappers
8 ounce	package rice vermicelli noodles, cooked according to package instructions
1 large	carrot, julienned thinly
3 tablespoons	Thai basil, chopped
3 tablespoons	fresh mint leaves, chopped
3 tablespoons	fresh cilantro, chopped
4 leaves	Romaine lettuce, chopped
1/2 cup	San-J Thai Peanut Sauce

In a small saucepan, poach the shrimp until pink throughout. Drain and cool. Cut each shrimp in half lengthwise and set aside. Fill a large bowl with warm water. Dip one wrapper in the warm water for 10 seconds to soften. Drain the wrapper of excess water and place it flat on a cutting board. In a row across the center of the wrapper, place 2 shrimp halves, a handful of vermicelli, carrots, basil, mint, cilantro and lettuce, leaving about 2 inches uncovered on each side. Fold the uncovered sides inward, then tightly roll the wrapper. Repeat with the remaining rolls to make 8 rolls total. Heat the San-J Thai Peanut Sauce, if desired, by placing the sauce in a microwaveable bowl and heat on medium for 1 minute.

MAKES 4 APPETIZER SERVINGS.

Scallion Cakes with San-J Thai Peanut Sauce

These very intriguing Asian cakes are excellent when paired with beef or chicken satay.

Ingredients

5 cups	flour
1 1/2 cups	boiling water
1 1/2 tablespoons	cold water
	salt and pepper to taste
4 ounces	unsalted butter or lard, softened
2 large	bunches green onions, thinly sliced (about 30)
	vegetable oil for frying
3/4 cup	San-J Thai Peanut Sauce

Sift the flour into a large mixing bowl and add the boiling water, mixing well. Add the cold water and knead the dough to form a firm ball. Cover and let stand for 15 minutes.

Place the dough on a lightly oiled surface. Knead several more times and then divide into 6 equal portions. Roll out each portion into a 7-inch circle, using a lightly oiled rolling pin. Season each round with salt and pepper to taste. Spread each round with the softened butter or lard. Sprinkle about 1/4 cup of the sliced onions on each round. Roll each round to form a cylinder and then roll each cylinder into a ball. Roll each ball again until each forms a cake that is approximately 6 inches in diameter.

Heat a heavy, flat frying pan until hot. Add 2 tablespoons of vegetable oil. Reduce the heat to low. Fry each cake for 8 minutes, turning once after 4 minutes, until golden brown. Drain the cakes on paper towels. To serve, place each cake on an individual appetizer plate and drizzle with 2 tablespoons of San-J Thai Peanut Sauce. Serve immediately.

MAKES 6 APPETIZER SERVINGS.

Sesame Honey Chicken Wings

This American classic takes an Asian twist with the addition of San-J Tamari Sesame Salad Dressing.
Honey also gives these crispy chicken wings a warm sweetness that your guests will be unable to resist.

Ingredients

1/4 cup	clover honey
1 cup	San-J Tamari Sesame Salad Dressing
3 pounds	chicken wings, cleaned and small tips discarded

In a small saucepan on low heat, whisk the honey and the San-J Tamari Sesame Salad Dressing until well-mixed. Stir for 2 minutes over low heat. Remove from the heat and cool. Place the chicken wings in a large resealable plastic bag and pour the honey mixture into the bag. Seal and shake well to coat the chicken wings. Place in the refrigerator and marinate at least 2 hours or overnight.

Shake off the excess marinade and place the chicken wings in a single layer on a baking sheet. Position the baking sheet in a preheated 400°F oven for 40 minutes, or until cooked through. To give the chicken added crispness, place the chicken wings under a broiler for 2 minutes on each side.

MAKES 10 APPETIZER SERVINGS.

Classic Asian Spring Rolls

Crunchy and full of flavor, these spring rolls have a pork and prawn filling that is hard to beat. The San-J Thai Peanut Sauce is an essential accompaniment to these scrumptious appetizers.

Ingredients

2 tablespoons	vegetable oil
1/2 small	white onion, finely chopped
1 small	carrot, grated
2 teaspoons	fresh ginger, grated
2 cloves	garlic, minced
8 ounces	large prawns, shelled and minced
6 ounces	fresh ground pork
4 ounces	fresh bean sprouts, cut into 1-inch lengths
2 teaspoons	San-J Tamari
2 teaspoons	fresh cilantro, minced
2 packages	spring roll wrappers
1	egg, beaten
	vegetable oil for frying
1 cup	San-J Thai Peanut Sauce

In a large sauté pan, heat the 2 tablespoons vegetable oil over medium heat. Add the onion, carrot, and ginger and stir-fry until softened, about 4 minutes. Add the garlic, prawns, pork, and bean sprouts. Stir-fry on medium-high heat for 2 to 3 minutes. Remove from the heat and add the San-J Tamari and cilantro. Mix well to combine and set aside to cool.

Place 1 spring roll wrapper on a clean surface. Spread 1 tablespoon of the filling across one end of the wrapper, leaving a border of 1/2-inch on each side. Partially roll up the wrapper, leaving about 1/4 of the wrapper open. Brush the remaining open wrapper with the beaten egg and roll up the rest of the way. Repeat this process with the remaining filling and wrappers.

In a deep fryer or large, heavy-bottomed skillet, pour 2 to 3 inches of vegetable oil and preheat the oil to 350°F. Fry the spring rolls, a few at a time, until golden and cooked through. Do not crowd the spring rolls in the pan while frying, otherwise the spring rolls will become soggy. Drain the spring rolls on paper towels and serve with the San-J Thai Peanut Sauce for dipping.

MAKES ABOUT 48 SPRING ROLLS.

Lemony Red Jacket Potatoes

These potatoes are easy and delicious. The San-J Sweet & Tangy sauce gives them a nice flavorful brightness and the green of the minced chives contrasts beautifully with the red jackets of the creamy potatoes.

Ingredients

10 medium	red potatoes, cut into fourths
2 cloves	garlic, minced
1 tablespoon	extra virgin olive oil
	salt and pepper to taste
1 tablespoon	San-J Sweet & Tangy Sauce
1/2 teaspoon	fresh lemon juice
1 tablespoon	fresh chives, minced

Preheat the oven to 450°F. In a medium mixing bowl, combine the potatoes, garlic, olive oil, salt and pepper until the potatoes are well-coated. Place the potatoes in a single layer on a nonstick baking sheet and bake in the oven for 30 to 40 minutes, or until tender. Brush with the San-J Sweet & Tangy Sauce 10 minutes before removing the potatoes from the oven. Remove the potatoes from the oven and spoon them onto a large serving platter. Sprinkle the potatoes with the fresh lemon juice and chives and toss lightly. Serve immediately.

MAKES 4 SERVINGS.

Shiitake Mushrooms, Pea Pods & Water Chestnuts

Shiitake mushrooms give this dish a depth of character that is supplemented by San-J's Tamari.
The water chestnuts and bean sprouts provide complementary tastes and textures.

Ingredients

1 tablespoon	vegetable oil
1 teaspoon	toasted sesame oil
1/4 pound	fresh shiitake mushrooms, sliced, with stems removed
1/4 pound	fresh oyster mushrooms, sliced
2 teaspoons	light brown sugar
1/4 cup	dry sherry or sake
2 tablespoons	San-J Tamari
1 pound	sugar snap peas, trimmed
2 cups	fresh bean sprouts, cleaned
8 ounce	can sliced water chestnuts, drained

In a medium sauté pan, heat the oils on medium-high heat. Add the mushrooms and sauté until they just begin to brown. Add the sugar, sherry or sake and the San-J Tamari, mixing well to combine. Cook and stir for 1 minute and then add the sugar snap peas. Cover, reduce the heat to low, and steam the peas for 2 minutes until they are tender-crisp. Add the bean sprouts and water chestnuts and sauté until most of the liquid has evaporated.

MAKES 4 SERVINGS.

Baked Szechuan Tofu with Ginger Green Beans

Spicy and balanced, this flavorful dish combines the snap of tender-crisp green beans
with the creamy solidity of marinated tofu.

Ingredients

14 ounces	firm tofu, drained
2 tablespoons	San-J Szechuan Sauce
1/2 pound	fresh green beans, cleaned and trimmed
1 teaspoon	vegetable oil
2 cloves	garlic, thinly sliced
1 tablespoon	fresh ginger, minced
1/2 teaspoon	San-J Szechuan Sauce

Cut the drained tofu into 1-inch cubes and place in a medium mixing bowl. Add 2 tablespoons of the San-J Szechuan Sauce and blend lightly until all of the sauce has been incorporated into the tofu. Cover tightly and marinate for 30 minutes. Prepare a 1 1/2 quart ovenproof baking dish by coating it lightly with nonstick cooking spray. Pour the tofu and sauce into the dish and bake uncovered at 350°F for 45 minutes.

While the tofu is baking, use a steamer rack to steam the green beans over boiling water until the beans are just tender-crisp. Set aside.

In a large sauté pan, heat the oil for 1 minute and add the garlic and ginger. Mix well and cook and stir for 2 minutes until the garlic and ginger are soft. Add the steamed green beans and baked tofu and mix well with the garlic and ginger. Add 1/2 teaspoon of the San-J Szechuan Sauce and toss again to coat the ingredients with the sauce. Heat just until all ingredients are warmed together and serve immediately.

MAKES 4 SERVINGS.

O-Hitashi (SPINACH WITH SESAME SEEDS)

Each bite of this easy spinach dish is full of healthful goodness. San-J's Tamari is the perfect foil for the strong flavors of the spinach and the mild sesame seeds.

Ingredients

1 pound	fresh spinach, cleaned and stems removed
3 tablespoons	San-J Tamari
2 tablespoons	water
1 tablespoon	toasted sesame seeds
	salt to taste

In a large saucepan or double boiler, bring 6 cups of water to a boil over high heat. Blanch the spinach by placing the leaves in the boiling water, pushing the leaves under the water completely. Cook for 20 seconds. Remove, drain, and cool under cold running water. Squeeze the excess water out of the spinach by hand and place in a bowl.

In a small bowl, combine the San-J Tamari and water. Pour onto the spinach. Sprinkle the spinach with the sesame seeds, salt to taste and serve.

MAKES 4 SERVINGS.

Swiss Chard with Garlic, Lemon and Tamari

San-J Tamari brings a surprisingly delicate bite to this classic Italian recipe.

Ingredients

2 tablespoons	extra virgin olive oil
4 cloves	garlic, sliced very thinly
2 large	bunches chard or other dark leafy greens, thick stems removed, roughly chopped
1/4 teaspoon	dried red pepper flakes
1/2 teaspoon	fresh lemon zest
1 teaspoon	San-J Tamari
2 teaspoons	fresh lemon juice
1 teaspoon	extra virgin olive oil

In a large sauté pan, heat 2 tablespoons of the oil and garlic over medium-high heat just until the garlic is golden. Add the chard and coat with the garlic and oil, mixing lightly. Add the red pepper flakes, lemon zest and the San-J Tamari and toss to coat. Continue stirring until the chard has softened and darkened in color, about 3 minutes. Transfer the chard to a colander and, using tongs, gently squeeze the chard to remove any excess liquid. Return the chard to the pan and sprinkle with the lemon juice and remaining olive oil. Serve immediately.

MAKES 4 SERVINGS.

Vinaigrette Grilled Vegetables

The consummate accompaniment to a barbecued meal, these grilled vegetables are sure to delight.
Use any seasonal vegetables on hand for added variation.

Ingredients

1 1/2 cups	extra virgin olive oil
6 cloves	garlic, minced
1/2 teaspoon	ground black pepper
1 teaspoon	salt
1/2 teaspoon	dried red pepper flakes
2 pounds	eggplant, sliced into rounds 3/4-inch thick
3 pounds	red bell peppers, seeded and cut into wide spears
2 pounds	zucchini, sliced 3/4-inch thick
6 large	portobello mushrooms, cleaned and cut in half
2 large	red onions, sliced into rounds 3/4-inch thick
	San-J Tamari Vinaigrette Salad Dressing
1/4 cup	green onions, thinly sliced

Combine the olive oil, garlic and seasonings in a small bowl and mix well. Place the eggplant, red peppers, zucchini, mushrooms and red onions in a large shallow dish. Pour the olive oil mixture over the vegetables and allow the flavors to marinate for at least 1 hour.

Preheat an indoor or outdoor grill to medium-high heat. Spray the grill with a nonstick cooking spray to prevent the vegetables from sticking to the grill. Grill each kind of vegetable separately in batches or all at once, depending on the size of the grill. Remove the vegetables as they become cooked through and softened, but do not allow the vegetables to dry out. Arrange the vegetables on a large serving platter and drizzle generously with the San-J Tamari Vinaigrette Salad Dressing. Garnish with the sliced green onions.

MAKES 10 SERVINGS.

Szechuan Eggplant Stir-Fry

The combination of the San-J Szechuan and Teriyaki Sauces creates a most satisfying vegetarian main course.
You will not miss the meat in this delightful vegetable medley.

Ingredients

2 cloves	garlic, minced
1 tablespoon	extra virgin olive oil
2 medium	Japanese eggplants, peeled and roughly chopped
1 large	yellow onion, cut into bite-sized wedges
2 medium	zucchini, roughly chopped
2	red bell peppers, seeded and roughly chopped
	salt and pepper to taste
2 tablespoons	San-J Szechuan Sauce
3 tablespoons	San-J Teriyaki Sauce
1/4 cup	dry white wine or sake
1/4 cup	fresh green onions, thinly sliced
6 cups	steamed white rice

In a large sauté pan or wok, heat the garlic in the oil over medium-high heat until the garlic begins to soften, about 1 minute. Add the eggplants, onion, zucchini and bell peppers and season lightly with salt and pepper. Stir-fry until the vegetables begin to soften, about 3 to 4 minutes. Add the San-J sauces and white wine or sake, stir well to combine and cook for an additional 3 minutes, or until the sauce begins to thicken. Remove from the heat. Garnish with green onions and serve over white rice.

MAKES 6 SERVINGS.

Horenso Peanuts Aé (SPINACH WITH PEANUT SAUCE)

This is a very classic Japanese preparation that combines the earthiness of fresh spinach with the sweet bite of roasted peanuts.

Ingredients

1 pound	fresh spinach, cleaned
1/2 cup	San-J Thai Peanut Sauce
2 tablespoons	roasted peanuts, finely chopped

Blanch the spinach by placing the leaves in a large pot of boiling water, pushing the leaves under the water completely. Cook for 20 seconds. Remove, drain, and cool under cold running water. Squeeze the excess water out of the spinach by hand and place in a medium serving bowl. Add the San-J Thai Peanut Sauce and toss lightly but thoroughly to coat. Garnish with the chopped peanuts.

MAKES 4 SERVINGS.

Teriyaki Vegetable Fajita Wraps

Grilled vegetables are a healthy and tasty filling for wraps. The Asian flavoring adds a delicious tang
to these wraps. Serve with additional San-J Teriyaki Sauce for dipping.

Ingredients

1/4 cup	fresh lime juice
2 cloves	garlic, minced
1 cup	San-J Teriyaki Sauce
1 tablespoon	fresh cilantro, minced
2 large	red bell peppers, seeded and sliced into strips
2 large	yellow bell peppers, seeded and sliced into strips
2 large	green bell peppers, seeded and sliced into strips
2 large	red onions, sliced into rounds 1/2-inch thick
3 medium	zucchini, sliced into 1/2-inch thick rounds
8 large	flour tortillas
2 cups	steamed white rice
1 cup	Monterey Jack cheese, shredded

In a medium mixing bowl, combine the lime juice, garlic, San-J Teriyaki Sauce and cilantro. Toss
to mix well. Place all of the vegetables in a very large mixing bowl and pour the San-J Teriyaki Sauce
mixture over the vegetables. Toss again to combine. Cover and marinate for at least one hour.

On a lightly greased grill over medium-high heat, grill the vegetables in batches until they have
softened, about 6 to 10 minutes. Do not allow them to burn as they grill.

To assemble the wraps, soften the tortillas by wrapping them in a damp paper towel and
microwaving them for 30 seconds on high heat. Stuff each tortilla evenly with the grilled teriyaki
vegetables. Top each wrap with white rice and garnish with cheese.

MAKES 8 SERVINGS.

Shanghai Potatoes

East meets West in these delightful potato cakes. Serve them with Grilled Lemon Herb Chicken (p.65) or any seafood entrée.

Ingredients

1 pound	russet potatoes, peeled, boiled, and drained well
3 ounces	frozen peas, thawed
1 tablespoon	fresh cilantro, minced
1 teaspoon	curry powder
1 teaspoon	salt
1/4 teaspoon	ground black pepper
1 tablespoon	San-J Thai Peanut Sauce
1	egg, beaten
6 ounces	fresh white bread crumbs
	vegetable oil

Drain the potatoes as much as possible. While still hot, mash the boiled potatoes until they are light and fluffy. Add the peas, cilantro, curry powder, salt, pepper and San-J Thai Peanut Sauce, gently combining all ingredients. Using your hands, take a portion of the potatoes about the size of a small ice cream scoop and form it into a flattened cake. Repeat with the remaining potatoes to make about 10 cakes. Dip each cake into the beaten egg and then cover with bread crumbs. Prepare a large skillet by heating the oil until hot, but not smoking. Place 2 to 3 cakes in the oiled skillet and fry over medium-high heat for about 3 minutes on each side, or until browned and warm throughout. Serve immediately.

MAKES 5 SERVINGS.

Sweet Mashed Potatoes with Toasted Walnuts

A perfect accompaniment to roasted chicken or pork, this deliciously sweet dish is made even better with the crunchy addition of toasted nuts.

Ingredients

4 large	sweet potatoes, roasted and skinned
1/4 cup	orange juice
4 tablespoons	butter
2 tablespoons	San-J Tamari
1/4 cup	walnuts, chopped

In a mixing bowl, mash the roasted sweet potatoes and add the orange juice, butter and the San-J Tamari. Mix well to combine. Place in a glass baking dish and sprinkle with chopped walnuts. Place under the broiler for about 3 minutes or until the walnuts are toasted.

MAKES 6 SERVINGS.

Ginger Bok Choy with Shiitake Mushrooms

Ginger adds an aromatic intensity to the stir-fried vegetables in this lovely Japanese favorite.

Ingredients

2 pounds	fresh bok choy
1 tablespoon	extra virgin olive oil
2 tablespoons	fresh ginger, grated
1/2 teaspoon	dried red pepper flakes
2 cloves	garlic, minced
8 ounces	fresh shiitake mushrooms, stems removed, sliced
1/8 cup	chicken broth
1 tablespoon	toasted sesame oil
2 tablespoons	San-J Tamari
1/8 cup	toasted sliced almonds

Trim off the root ends of the bok choy and discard. Wash thoroughly and drain well. Separate the leaves and the stems. Chop the stems into 1-inch pieces. Chop the green leaves into pieces about 2-inches in length.

In a large skillet over medium-high heat, heat the olive oil. Add the ginger, red pepper flakes and garlic. Stir-fry for 3 minutes. Add the mushrooms and chopped bok choy stems and reduce the heat to medium, cooking for 3 minutes. Add the chicken broth and bok choy leaves and cook for another 2 minutes. Remove from the heat and add the sesame oil and the San-J Tamari. Stir and toss to combine. Sprinkle with the sliced almonds to garnish. Serve immediately.

MAKES 4 SERVINGS.

Kabocha with Tamari Sake Broth

Buttery soft kabocha meets a sophisticated Tamari sake broth with an irresistible result!

Ingredients

1 pound	kabocha squash, stem and seeds removed, unpeeled
1/4 cup	San-J Tamari
1/4 cup	sake
1/4 cup	water
2 tablespoons	sugar

Cut the kabocha squash into 1-inch, bite-sized pieces. In a small mixing bowl, whisk together the San-J Tamari, sake, water and sugar. Place the kabocha in a medium saucepan and pour the Tamari mixture over the squash. Cover, bring the squash to a boil, and simmer for 20 minutes or until squash is tender and cooked through. Serve hot or at room temperature.

MAKES 4 SERVINGS.

Roasted Beet Salad

A tangibly beautiful composition of roasted fresh beets and zesty mustard dressing.
Serve with a beef, pork or lamb entrée.

Ingredients

1 1/2 pounds	red beets, stems trimmed to 1-inch
1 tablespoon	extra virgin olive oil
1/2 teaspoon	salt
2 tablespoons	San-J Tamari Mustard Salad Dressing
1 head	bibb or butter lettuce, leaves separated
2 tablespoons	toasted almonds, thinly sliced

Preheat the oven to 400°F. Rinse the beets and clean any debris from the beets. Place the beets in a large, ovenproof baking dish and toss with the olive oil until thoroughly coated. Season with the salt and toss again. Cover the beets securely with aluminum foil and roast until tender, about 45 minutes to 1 hour. Remove from the oven and set aside to cool.

Peel the cooled beets and cut them into quarters. In a large mixing bowl, toss the beets with the San-J Tamari Mustard Salad Dressing until they are very well-coated. Cover the beets loosely and let stand for 30 minutes or up to 1 hour so that the flavors will marry. Arrange the lettuce leaves on a decorative platter and cover the leaves with the beets. Garnish with the almond slices.

MAKES 4 SERVINGS.

Apollonian Asian Salad

Greece meets Asia in this lively and colorful salad.

Ingredients

1 head	leaf lettuce, torn into bite-sized pieces
2 large	ripe tomatoes, cubed
2 large	cucumbers, sliced
1/2 medium	red onion, chopped
1 cup	feta cheese, crumbled
1/2 cup	Greek kalamata olives, pitted
1/2 cup	San-J Tamari Vinaigrette Salad Dressing

Assemble the salad in layers on 4 individual salad plates. Place a layer of lettuce pieces on each plate, distributing the leaves evenly. Scatter the cubed tomatoes over the lettuce. Place slices of the cucumbers on each plate and spread the chopped red onion over all. Finish with a layer of crumbled feta cheese over each salad. Garnish each serving with the Greek olives. Drizzle the San-J Tamari Vinaigrette Salad Dressing lightly over the top of each salad and chill the salads in the refrigerator for 30 minutes prior to serving.

MAKES 4 SERVINGS.

Indonesian Gado Gado Salad

This traditional Indonesian dish combines fresh vegetables with the creamy flavor of San-J Tamari Peanut Salad Dressing. The salad may be served as an accompaniment or, with the addition of chicken or tofu, can be a fulfilling entrée.

Ingredients

1 cup	Yukon Gold potatoes, chopped
1 cup	fresh broccoli florets (you may substitute frozen, thawed florets)
1 cup	fresh sugar snap peas, trimmed
1/2 head	green cabbage, shredded
2 cups	baby spinach leaves, cleaned
1 cup	fresh mung bean sprouts, cleaned
1 large	red tomato, chopped
1 large	fresh cucumber, sliced
1 cup	San-J Tamari Peanut Salad Dressing, divided
1 large	hard-boiled egg, sliced

Prepare the potatoes, broccoli and sugar snap peas by steaming them over boiling water in a large saucepan for 15 minutes, or until tender. Set aside to cool. On a large serving platter, arrange a layer of shredded cabbage and spinach leaves. In a large mixing bowl, combine the potatoes, broccoli, sugar snap peas, bean sprouts, tomato, cucumber and 1/2 cup of San-J Tamari Peanut Salad Dressing. Toss lightly to combine. Spread the vegetables and dressing over the top of the cabbage and spinach leaves. Place the egg slices on top. Drizzle the remaining San-J Tamari Peanut Salad Dressing on top of the salad.

MAKES 8 SERVINGS.

Cilantro & Mint Cabbage Coleslaw

Red and green vegetables with exciting crunch and flavor are dressed up with the San-J Tamari Peanut Salad Dressing. Although this salad is simple to prepare, it's quite impressive upon presentation.

Ingredients

2 cups	green cabbage, finely shredded
1 cup	red cabbage, finely shredded
1/2 cup	green onions, finely sliced
2	red bell peppers, seeded and finely sliced
1/4 cup	fresh cilantro, minced
1/4 cup	fresh mint, finely chopped
1/2 cup	San-J Tamari Peanut Salad Dressing
3 tablespoons	roasted peanuts, finely chopped

In a medium serving bowl, combine the cabbage, green onions, bell peppers, cilantro and mint. Toss thoroughly with the San-J Tamari Peanut Salad Dressing. Chill for several hours and garnish with the roasted peanuts.

MAKES 6 SERVINGS.

Sesame Green Vegetable Salad

Garden-fresh and very green, this salad is stunningly beautiful and delicious.

Ingredients

1 pound	sugar snap peas, trimmed
1 pound	small green beans, trimmed
1 pound	fresh broccoli florets, cleaned
1/2 cup	San-J Tamari Sesame Salad Dressing
2 tablespoons	fresh orange juice
1 tablespoon	grated orange zest
1 teaspoon	honey
1/4 cup	chives, thinly sliced
2 tablespoons	toasted sesame seeds

Steam the sugar snap peas by placing them in a basket over boiling water for approximately 10 minutes, or until tender-crisp. Plunge into iced water to stop the cooking process and retain the crispness. Remove the peas from the water, drain and cool. Steam the green beans and broccoli florets in the same manner, cool and set aside.

In a small mixing bowl, whisk together the San-J Tamari Sesame Salad Dressing, orange juice, orange zest and honey until well-blended and smooth. Allow the dressing to stand for at least 30 minutes to allow the flavors to marry.

In a large salad serving bowl, toss the cooled vegetables with the orange-sesame dressing. Sprinkle the chives and toasted sesame seeds over the salad and toss to combine. Serve immediately.

MAKES 6 SERVINGS.

Warm Winter Chicken Salad

Acting as a substantial salad entrée, this delightful combination of chicken, asparagus, potatoes, eggs and bacon is topped with a sparkling mustard dressing-perfect for a cold winter's evening.

Ingredients

4	boneless, skinless chicken breasts
	salt and pepper to taste
1/4 cup	dry white wine
1 bunch	fresh asparagus, trimmed
10 baby	red potatoes, cut in half and steamed
1/2 cup	San-J Tamari Mustard Salad Dressing, divided
3 cups	baby spinach leaves
2	hard-boiled eggs, sliced
6 slices	bacon, cooked until crispy and crumbled

Preheat the oven to 325°F. In a baking dish, season the chicken with salt and pepper and add the wine. Cover tightly with aluminum foil and bake for 30 minutes or until cooked through and no pink remains. Remove from the oven and let the chicken stand for 10 minutes. Shred the chicken and place in a medium bowl.

Steam the asparagus in a steamer basket over boiling water until tender-crisp, about 8 minutes. Drain and set aside to cool. Steam the potatoes in the same process for 15-20 minutes, or until tender. Drain and set aside to cool.

In a medium saucepan, heat the San-J Tamari Mustard Salad Dressing until warm. Pour 1/4 cup over the shredded chicken. Meanwhile, line a large serving platter with the spinach leaves, overlapping the leaves as necessary. Place the potatoes on top of the spinach. Layer the asparagus over the potatoes. Scatter the shredded chicken on top of the potatoes and asparagus and drizzle the remaining warm San-J Tamari Mustard Salad Dressing on top. Garnish with hard-boiled egg slices and crumbled bacon. Serve immediately.

MAKES 6 ENTRÉE SERVINGS.

Shrimp & Rice Vermicelli Salad

The cool, inviting flavors of fresh mint and cilantro perfectly accent the flavorful shrimp salad.
Serve on chilled plates on a warm summer day.

Ingredients

8 ounces	rice vermicelli noodles, cooked according to package instructions, and cooled
1 large	cucumber, peeled and julienned
1 large	carrot, peeled and julienned
1 large	tomato, cut into 12 wedges
24 medium	shrimp, shelled, deveined, poached and cooled
1/2 cup	San-J Tamari Vinaigrette Salad Dressing
1/4 cup	fresh mint leaves, minced
1/4 cup	fresh cilantro, minced

Divide the vermicelli noodles evenly among 4 large individual serving bowls. Place the cucumber pieces on top of the noodles. Cover with the carrot and add the tomato wedges to each bowl. Place the cooked shrimp on top of each salad. Drizzle each salad with the San-J Tamari Vinaigrette Salad Dressing, and garnish with minced mint and cilantro.

MAKES 4 SERVINGS.

Szechuan Beef Spinach Salad

This is a sophisticated wilted spinach salad that is nicely balanced by the sweetness of the peppers and the zingy flavor of the San-J Szechuan Sauce.

Ingredients

1 pound	sirloin steak, cut into bite-sized strips
1/2 cup	San-J Szechuan Sauce
1 tablespoon	vegetable oil
2	red bell peppers, seeded and roughly chopped
2	yellow onions, sliced
6 cups	baby spinach leaves, cleaned and dried
2 tablespoons	rice wine vinegar
6 tablespoons	extra virgin olive oil
1/4 teaspoon	salt
1/4 teaspoon	freshly ground black pepper
1/2 cup	roasted peanuts, chopped

Toss the steak strips with the San-J Szechuan Sauce in a large bowl or resealable plastic bag. Marinate for at least 1 hour or up to 3 hours. Heat the vegetable oil in a large skillet or wok over high heat. Add the steak strips and stir-fry for about 5 minutes, or until no longer red in the middle. Add the red bell peppers and onions and stir-fry for another 2 minutes.

Prepare 6 individual salad plates. Spread the spinach evenly among the plates. Remove the meat and vegetables from heat and, while still hot, place evenly over the spinach. Whisk together the rice wine vinegar, olive oil, salt and pepper and drizzle over each individual wilted spinach and beef salad. Garnish the salads with chopped peanuts.

MAKES 6 SERVINGS.

Sesame Prawns and Avocado Citrus Salad

This lovely salad is all about balanced texture. The jicama matchsticks add a wonderful crunch to the buttery softness of the avocado and the sweet mangos are a wonderful foil for the grilled prawns. The San-J Tamari Sesame Salad Dressing is the perfect accompaniment.

Ingredients

16	jumbo prawns, cleaned, deveined
1/2 cup	San-J Tamari Sesame Salad Dressing
2	firm-ripe mangoes, pits removed, peeled and julienned
1 large	jicama, peeled and julienned
2	ripe avocados, peeled, pitted and cut into bite-sized chunks
1/4 cup	San-J Tamari Sesame Salad Dressing
2 tablespoons	fresh lime juice

Place the prawns in a resealable plastic bag and add 1/2 cup of the San-J Tamari Sesame Salad Dressing. Seal and shake to combine. Marinate the prawns for 1 hour in the refrigerator.

Heat an indoor or outdoor grill to medium-high heat. Shake off any excess marinade from the prawns and place the marinated prawns on the grill. Cook until the prawns are opaque and pink, about 2 minutes per side. Set the prawns aside to cool.

In a large mixing bowl, combine the mango, jicama, avocado, 1/4 cup San-J Tamari Sesame Salad Dressing and the lime juice. Mix very gently to combine. Place equal portions of the salad on 4 individual chilled salad plates and top each with 4 jumbo grilled prawns.

MAKES 4 SERVINGS.

Chicken Curry Salad

This cool chicken salad is perfect on any hot summer evening.

Ingredients

4	boneless, skinless chicken breasts, cooked and cubed
1	tart apple, cored and chopped
6	green onions, finely sliced
3	celery ribs, finely sliced
1/2 cup	golden raisins
1/2 cup	almonds, sliced
1 cup	mayonnaise
2 tablespoons	curry powder
1 teaspoon	cayenne pepper
1 tablespoon	San-J Tamari
1 teaspoon	fresh lemon juice
4 cups	red lettuce leaves, cleaned and drained

In a large mixing bowl, combine the cubed chicken, apple, green onions, celery and raisins. Mix well. Add the almonds and mix again. Prepare the dressing by whisking together the mayonnaise, curry powder, cayenne pepper, San-J Tamari and lemon juice.

Add the dressing to the chicken mixture and blend well with a soft spatula. Cover tightly and refrigerate for 1 hour or up to 4 hours. To serve, arrange the red lettuce leaves on 6 individual salad plates. Spoon the chicken salad over the lettuce in equal portions. Chill for 30 minutes and serve. Note: You may also prepare the salad and use it as a filling for pita pockets or other sturdy sandwich breads.

MAKES 6 SERVINGS.

Summertime Sliced Heirloom Tomato Salad

"Summertime Heirloom" tomatoes can be used to ensure the most fantastic flavor and color in this salad.
Japanese cucumbers are a crisp, cool textural contrast to the meaty, sweet tomatoes.
The fresh basil is the perfect herb for this easy salad.

Ingredients

3 large	ripe tomatoes (preferably "Summertime Heirloom"), peeled
2 medium	fresh Japanese cucumbers, peeled (you may substitute standard cucumbers, if desired)
1/4 large	red onion, thinly sliced
1 cup	fresh basil leaves
1/4 cup	San-J Tamari Mustard Salad Dressing

Cut the tomatoes into 1/4-inch thick slices. Cut the cucumbers into 1/4-inch thick slices. On a large platter, arrange the tomatoes evenly to form a bottom layer. Top with a layer of the cucumber slices. Arrange the red onion slices over the cucumbers. Finish with a sprinkling of basil leaves. Dress the salad with the San-J Tamari Mustard Salad Dressing. Allow the salad to stand for at least 10 minutes to allow the flavors to become absorbed and serve immediately.

MAKES 6 SERVINGS.

Tamari Vinaigrette Three Bean Salad

If only all delicious dishes were this uncomplicated! This salad has been a family favorite for years, but the San-J Tamari Vinaigrette Salad Dressing adds a new level of interest to the rest of the flavors. You may double the recipe for large crowds.

Ingredients

14 ounce	can cut green beans, drained
15 ounce	can red kidney beans, drained
14 ounce	can garbanzo beans (chickpeas), drained
2	celery ribs, cleaned and sliced
1	green bell pepper, seeded and finely chopped
1/4 cup	white onion, finely chopped
1 cup	San-J Tamari Vinaigrette Salad Dressing
	freshly ground black pepper to taste

Combine the green beans, kidney beans, garbanzo beans and celery in a large serving bowl. Toss well to combine. Add the green pepper and white onion and toss again. Pour the San-J Tamari Vinaigrette Salad Dressing over the vegetables and toss thoroughly to incorporate all of the dressing. Sprinkle with the black pepper to taste. Cover tightly with plastic wrap and refrigerate for at least 6 hours or up to 24 hours. Serve chilled.

MAKES 6 SERVINGS.

Sesame & Cilantro Cabbage Mélange

*The word, "mélange" is French for "medley," which describes this salad perfectly.
Use this salad as an accompaniment to almost any entrée and wait for surprising compliments.*

Ingredients

2 medium	Japanese cucumbers, thinly sliced (you may substitute 1 large standard cucumber, if desired)
8	red radishes, cleaned, tops removed, thinly sliced
3/4 cup	San-J Tamari Sesame Salad Dressing, divided
4 cups	napa cabbage, finely shredded
4 cups	red cabbage, finely shredded
1/2 cup	green onions, finely sliced
1/4 cup	fresh cilantro, minced
3 tablespoons	toasted sesame seeds

In a medium mixing bowl, combine the cucumber slices, radish slices, and 1/4 cup of the San-J Sesame Salad Dressing. Cover loosely and let the vegetables stand for at least 1 hour to allow the flavors to marry.

Shortly before serving, combine the cabbages in a large serving bowl. Place the cucumber and radish slices on top. Pour the remaining San-J Tamari Sesame Salad Dressing over the salad and toss thoroughly to combine. Garnish with the green onions, cilantro and sesame seeds.

MAKES 8 SERVINGS.

Chilled Thai Noodles

This noodle dish is refreshing and simple to make, with the perfect combination of crunch and color. You may want to add shredded chicken to make this a main dish or simply serve as a side to your favorite Asian-style meat or tofu dish. This recipe is also perfect for large parties or picnics.

Ingredients

1 cup	San-J Tamari Peanut Salad Dressing, divided
1 pound	angel hair pasta, cooked al dente and drained
8	green onions, finely sliced
3 medium	carrots, peeled and julienned
1	fresh cucumber, seeded and julienned
1 cup	red cabbage, finely shredded
1 cup	unsalted peanuts, chopped
2 tablespoons	fresh cilantro, minced

In a large serving bowl or serving platter, combine 1/2 cup of the San-J Tamari Peanut Salad Dressing with the angel hair pasta. Toss or mix thoroughly to completely incorporate the dressing into the noodles. Cover and set aside for at least 30 minutes.

To assemble, add the green onions, carrots, cucumber and remaining dressing to the marinated noodles. Toss lightly. Add the red cabbage and toss again. Shortly before serving, add the unsalted peanuts and cilantro and mix thoroughly. Serve immediately.

MAKES 6 SERVINGS.

Farfalle with Tamari Mustard & Artichokes

Artichokes and pasta are an Italian pairing, however the San-J Tamari Mustard Salad Dressing offers a distinctly Asian cast to this special entrée. Serve with chilled white wine and baguettes of sourdough bread.

Ingredients

1 tablespoon	extra virgin olive oil
1 pound	farfalle pasta
2 - 14 ounce	cans artichoke hearts, drained and chopped
1 cup	frozen green peas, thawed
1 large	red bell pepper, finely sliced
14 ounce	can black olives, drained
3 tablespoons	fresh flat-leaf parsley, finely chopped
1 cup	San-J Tamari Mustard Salad Dressing

Bring 7 to 8 cups of water to a boil in a large stockpot or saucepan. Add the olive oil to the water and drop in the pasta while the water is boiling vigorously. Stir and cook, uncovered, until the pasta gives to the bite, al dente style. Drain the pasta and keep warm.

In a large mixing bowl, combine the artichoke hearts, peas, red pepper, olives, parsley and San-J Tamari Mustard Salad Dressing. Toss lightly to incorporate the dressing into all of the vegetables. Add the pasta and toss again. Serve immediately.

MAKES 8 SERVINGS.

Oyako Donburi (CHICKEN & EGG WITH RICE)

This is a wonderfully soothing rice dish, guaranteed to put a smile on the face of everyone at the table.

Ingredients

1 tablespoon	vegetable oil
1 large	white onion, thinly sliced
5	fresh or reconstituted shiitake mushrooms, thinly sliced
1/2 pound	boneless, skinless chicken breasts, thinly sliced
1/8 teaspoon	salt
1 1/2 cups	second dashi or chicken stock
1 teaspoon	sugar
4 tablespoons	mirin
4 tablespoons	San-J Tamari
4 large	eggs, lightly beaten
1/4 cup	frozen green peas, thawed
4	mitsuba sprigs, root removed, leaves roughly chopped (optional)
4 cups	steamed Japanese rice

Place the oil in a medium sauté pan and cook the onion and mushrooms for 1 minute, stirring as the onion becomes translucent. Add the chicken and cook until it is golden, about 2 minutes. Add the salt, dashi or stock, sugar, mirin and San-J Tamari. Stir well to combine. Bring to a boil over medium-high heat. Pour the lightly beaten eggs into the hot mixture and add the green peas and mitsuba. Stir, cover and simmer until the eggs are cooked, about 1 to 2 minutes.

To serve, scoop the warm Japanese rice into 4 individual bowls and ladle the chicken and egg sauce over the top of the rice. Serve immediately and pass additional San-J Tamari at the table.

MAKES 4 SERVINGS.

Crunchy Chicken & Maifun Noodles

Look for maifun noodles in the specialty food aisle of your grocery store to add the extra crunch in this exciting dish.

Ingredients

4	boneless, skinless chicken breasts, cooked and diced
4 tablespoons	San-J Tamari Vinaigrette Salad Dressing
4 cups	green cabbage, thinly shredded
2 large	carrots, peeled and shredded
6 ounces	Chinese maifun noodles, crisped in hot oil
5	green onions, thinly sliced
2 tablespoons	toasted sesame seeds

Place the chicken in a resealable plastic bag and add the San-J Tamari Vinaigrette Salad Dressing. Marinate in the refrigerator for at least 15 minutes or up to 2 hours. In a large mixing bowl, combine the shredded green cabbage and shredded carrot, tossing well to combine thoroughly.

Prepare 4 individual plates for presentation. Evenly divide the crispy noodles and place 1 portion on each plate. Scatter the cabbage and carrots evenly over the noodles. Scoop equal portions of the marinated chicken onto the cabbage and carrots. Drizzle any remaining San-J Tamari Vinaigrette Salad Dressing over the chicken and noodles. Garnish with the green onions and sesame seeds.

MAKES 4 SERVINGS.

Japanese Buckwheat Noodles WITH TEMPURA VEGETABLES

This dish is perfection on a hot day. The cold noodles combined with the warm and crunchy tempura take your mind away from the oppressive heat of a Japanese summer. The coolness of the salty-sweet dipping sauce is the perfect accompaniment. Be creative and use your favorite vegetables in the tempura batter to personalize this tasty dish.

Dipping Sauce Ingredients

2 ounces	Japanese dried fish flakes (Kezuri-bushi)
1 cup	San-J Tamari
1 cup	mirin
1 tablespoon	sugar
3 cups	water
1 teaspoon	wasabi paste (optional)

Tempura Ingredients

2 1/4 cups	all-purpose flour, sifted
2 cups	iced water (this must be very cold)
1 extra large	egg, beaten
8	jumbo prawns, deveined, heads and shell removed, tails intact
	vegetables of your choice and season (see note below)
	vegetable oil for frying

Noodle Ingredients

14 ounces	dried soba noodles
4	spring onions, finely sliced

Prepare the dipping sauce by combining the first 5 sauce ingredients together in a small saucepan. Whisk gently over medium heat until the sauce boils. Cook and stir for 3 minutes. Reduce the heat and cook on medium-low for another 3 minutes. Decant (or strain) through a cheesecloth or paper towel. Place the sauce in a sealable plastic container and refrigerate to chill.

To make the tempura, place the sifted flour in a chilled, medium-sized mixing bowl. Combine the iced water and egg and pour over the flour. Stir just until combined. The tempura will be slightly lumpy. Do not whisk until smooth!

Pour the vegetable oil into a deep fryer or wok to a depth of 2 inches. Heat on high heat, using a thermometer to measure the heat of the oil. When the oil reaches 350°F, the oil is hot enough to be used for the tempura. Using an oven mitt or protective glove, dip a few of the prawns into the batter and place them in the hot oil. Add only a few pieces of fish to the oil at a time so that the temperature is not reduced and the fryer or wok does not become crowded. As the prawns turn golden brown and cook through, about 3 minutes total, remove them from the oil using a slotted spoon and drain on paper towels. Place the cooked prawns on a warm platter and keep warm.

Prepare the vegetable tempura in the same manner as the prawns by dipping your choice of vegetables into the batter and deep frying in small batches. Maintain the proper temperature and remove any extra batter that accumulates in the oil. Most vegetables will be cooked tender-crisp within 2 to 4 minutes, depending on the type of vegetables you choose and the size of each piece of tempura. Check the first piece of tempura by removing it from the oil and cutting it open to determine whether or not it is cooked as desired. If not fully cooked, increase the frying time for the remainder of the vegetables, testing the vegetables occasionally as the tempura fries. Remove the cooked tempura vegetables with a slotted spoon, drain and keep warm with the prawns.

Prepare the soba noodles as directed, cooking al dente according to the package instructions (about 5 minutes in boiling water). Drain and cool under cold running water.

To assemble, prepare 4 small, individual serving plates. Divide the cold noodles evenly among the plates. Sprinkle the noodles with the spring onions. Place the optional wasabi in a small bowl. On 4 additional accompanying small plates, divide the tempura prawns and vegetables among the plates. In 4 small bowls, divide the chilled dipping sauce. Provide chopsticks for each diner. Using the chopsticks, each diner may mix some wasabi in their dipping sauce for a little spiciness, as desired. Use chopsticks to dip the noodles and/or tempura in the dipping sauce.

MAKES 4 SERVINGS.

Note: Use sweet potatoes, carrots, asparagus (trimmed), whole green beans, zucchini, broccoli, cauliflower, winter squash and/or Asian eggplant - cut into 1/4-inch slices or florets. Plan on preparing enough vegetables to serve 6 to 8 vegetable pieces per person.

Szechuan Shrimp & Asparagus over Linguine

Springtime calls for tender asparagus and spicy Szechuan shrimp.
Plate this dish with a dusting of grated Romano cheese.

Ingredients

2 cloves	garlic, minced
8	crimini mushrooms, sliced
1 tablespoon	fresh ginger, grated
1 tablespoon	extra virgin olive oil
1 pound	fresh medium shrimp, peeled and deveined, tails intact
1	red bell pepper, seeded and sliced into strips
1/2 pound	fresh asparagus, trimmed and cut into 1-inch pieces
2 teaspoons	San-J Szechuan Sauce
1 cup	dry white wine
2 teaspoons	toasted sesame oil
2 teaspoons	San-J Tamari
	juice of 1/2 lemon
1 pound	linguine, cooked al dente, kept warm
2 tablespoons	flat-leaf parsley, minced
	Romano cheese for garnish

In a large sauté pan, cook and stir the garlic, mushrooms and ginger in olive oil over medium-high heat for 2 minutes. Add the shrimp and sauté just until pink, about 2 minutes. Remove the shrimp and keep warm on an ovenproof plate in the oven. Add the red bell pepper to the pan and sauté until crisp-tender.

Blanch the asparagus by steaming it for about 2 minutes in a deep saucepan over boiling water. Drain. Return the shrimp to the pan, add the blanched asparagus and add the San-J Szechuan Sauce, white wine, sesame oil, San-J Tamari and lemon juice. Stir the ingredients gently and heat through over low heat for 3 to 4 minutes. Add the cooked linguini and parsley to the pan and toss with the remaining ingredients. Dust the linguini and shrimp with Romano cheese and serve immediately.

MAKES 4 SERVINGS.

Stuffed Duo Peppers WITH SWEET & TANGY AU JUS

This beautiful red and orange pepper presentation is brought to life with the addition of the sweet and tangy au jus. Slow cooking completes the tender perfection.

Ingredients

1 pound	lean ground beef
1 medium	yellow onion, finely chopped
1 clove	garlic, minced
1 cup	uncooked white rice
	salt and pepper to taste
2 large	red bell peppers, cored and seeded
2 large	orange bell peppers, cored and seeded
1 cup	San-J Sweet & Tangy Sauce
2 cups	low-sodium beef broth
	water

In a large mixing bowl, combine the ground beef, onion, garlic, white rice, salt and pepper. Stuff each pepper evenly with the beef and rice combination, packing each pepper shell lightly. Place the stuffed peppers in a medium Dutch oven or high-sided baking pan. In a large mixing bowl, combine the San-J Sweet & Tangy Sauce and the beef broth. Whisk to combine well. Slowly pour the sauce and broth over the peppers. Add water, if necessary, to barely cover the peppers.

Heat the peppers and sauce over high heat until the sauce begins to boil. Reduce the heat and simmer, covered, for 3 hours, stirring every 30 minutes. Spoon the sauce over the peppers occasionally as the peppers cook. The sauce will thicken as the peppers cook. To serve, place 1 stuffed pepper on each of 4 individual plates and spoon the thickened sauce over each pepper.

MAKES 4 SERVINGS.

Creamy Cheese & Cracked Pepper Penne

Enjoy the rich creaminess of cheese and pasta all wrapped up in a Parmesan crust.

Ingredients

1/2 teaspoon	salt
1 pound	penne pasta
2 teaspoons	unsalted butter
2 teaspoons	all-purpose flour
1 cup	heavy cream
4 ounces	fontina cheese, grated
4 ounces	cream cheese, cubed
1/2 cup	Romano cheese, grated
1/4 cup	dairy sour cream
1 tablespoon	San-J Cracked Pepper Sauce
1 cup	sourdough or white bread crumbs
1/4 cup	Parmesan cheese, freshly grated

In a large pot, bring 4 quarts of water to a boil. Add the salt and the penne, stirring well to separate the individual pieces of pasta. Cook in boiling water until the pasta is slightly underdone, just before it becomes "al dente". Drain.

While the pasta is cooking, melt the butter in a small saucepan on medium-low heat and whisk in the flour until smooth. Cook and stir for about 1 minute to make a roux. Add the heavy cream and whisk again until combined. Bring to a boil, stirring constantly, and then reduce to a simmer for about 2 minutes. Watch the sauce carefully to avoid burning and stir often to ensure that it remains smooth.

Place the fontina, cream cheese, Romano, sour cream and the San-J Cracked Pepper Sauce in a large mixing bowl and combine thoroughly. Add the drained, hot pasta and the cream mixture.

Mix thoroughly to combine. Cover tightly with aluminum foil and let rest for 4 minutes.

While the pasta is resting, combine the bread crumbs and Parmesan cheese in a small bowl. Prepare a 9" x 13" rectangular baking pan by coating it lightly with nonstick cooking spray. Preheat the oven to 450°F. Pour the pasta and cheese into the prepared pan. Scatter the bread crumbs and cheese evenly over the pasta and cheese. Bake the pasta, uncovered, for 10 minutes, or until the crust is golden brown and the pasta is uniformly warm. Serve immediately.

MAKES 6 SERVINGS.

Chilled Petite Winter Vegetables WITH BROWN RICE

Colorful and naturally nutritious, this dish is a lovely accompaniment to roasted chicken or baked fish.

Ingredients

2 cups	small broccoli florets
1 cup	frozen green peas, thawed
3 cups	brown rice, cooked and cooled
3	green onions, thinly sliced
1 cup	carrots, julienned
1 cup	San-J Tamari Peanut Salad Dressing

Place the broccoli florets in a steamer basket in a deep saucepan. Add water and steam until tender-crisp, about 8 minutes. Set aside to cool. Place the peas, brown rice, green onions and carrots in a large mixing bowl. Add the cooled broccoli and toss the vegetables and rice to combine. Add the San-J Tamari Peanut Salad Dressing and toss again to fully incorporate the dressing with the vegetables.

Transfer the vegetables and rice to a serving platter and let stand, covered, for at least 1 hour or up to 2 hours to allow the flavors to marry. Add more San-J Tamari Peanut Salad Dressing at the table if you so desire.

MAKES 8 SERVINGS.

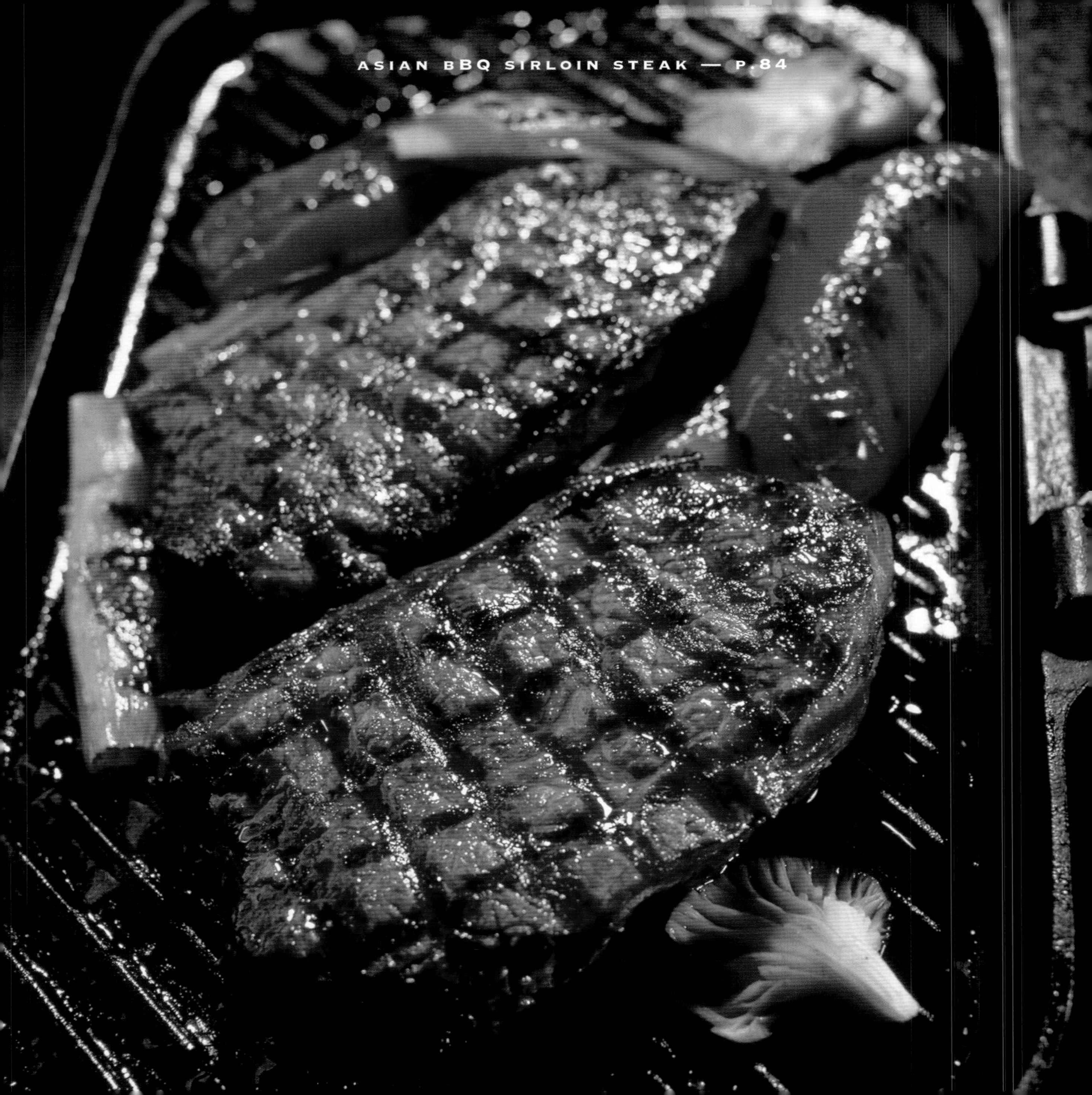

ASIAN BBQ SIRLOIN STEAK — P.84

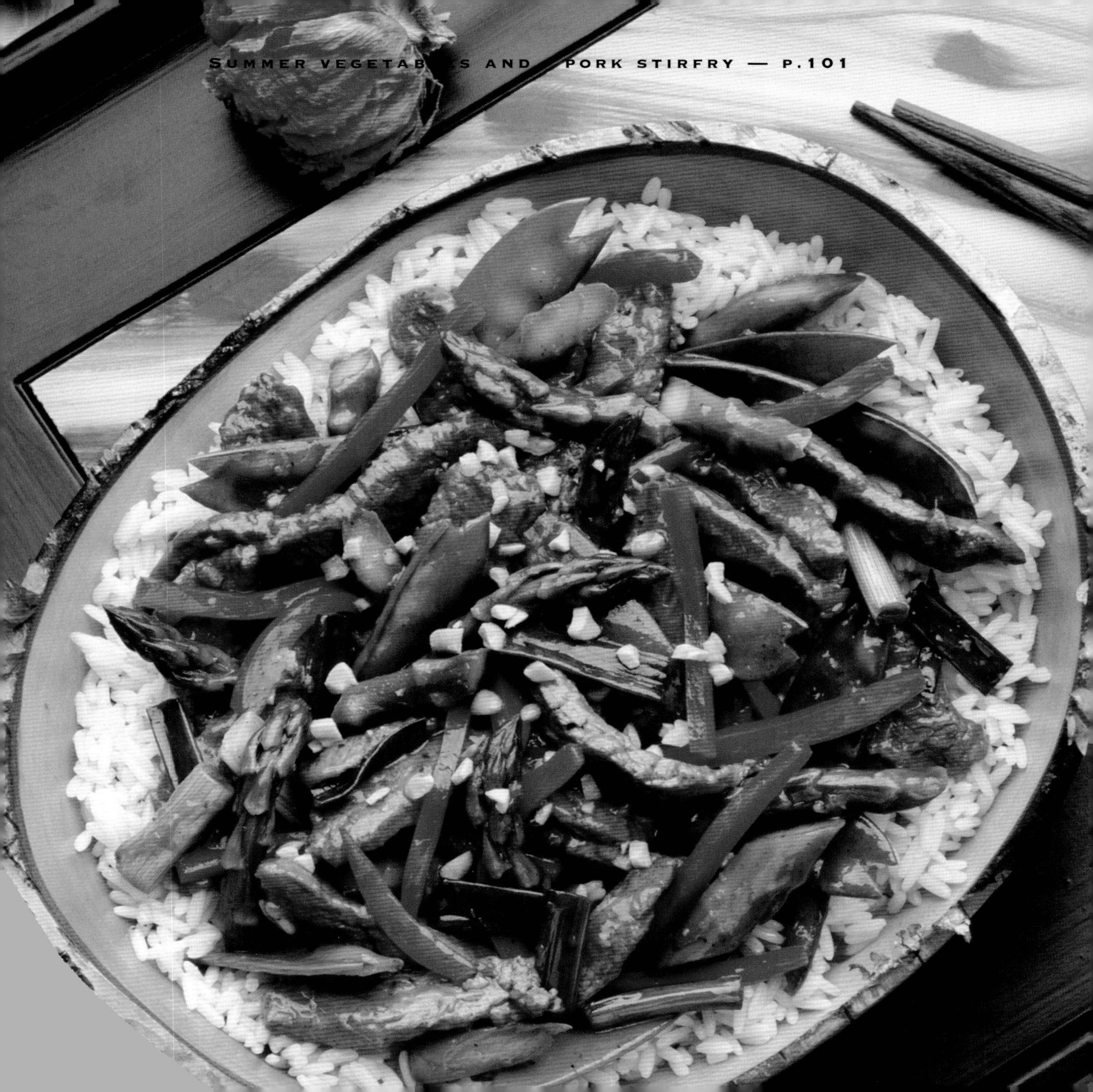

SUMMER VEGETABLES AND PORK STIRFRY — P.101

Honey and tamari chicken — p.67

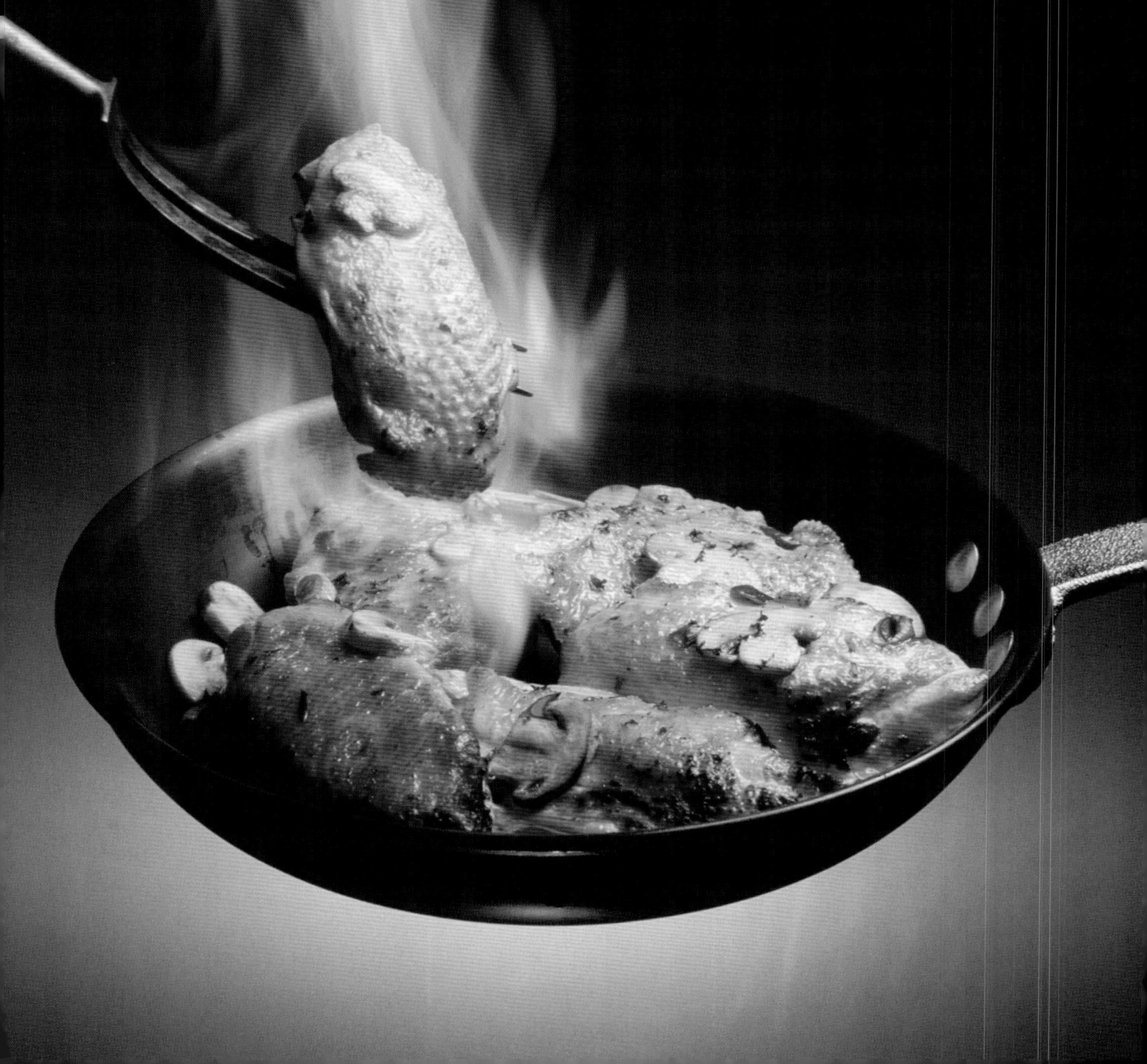

CHICKEN CURRY SALAD — P.42

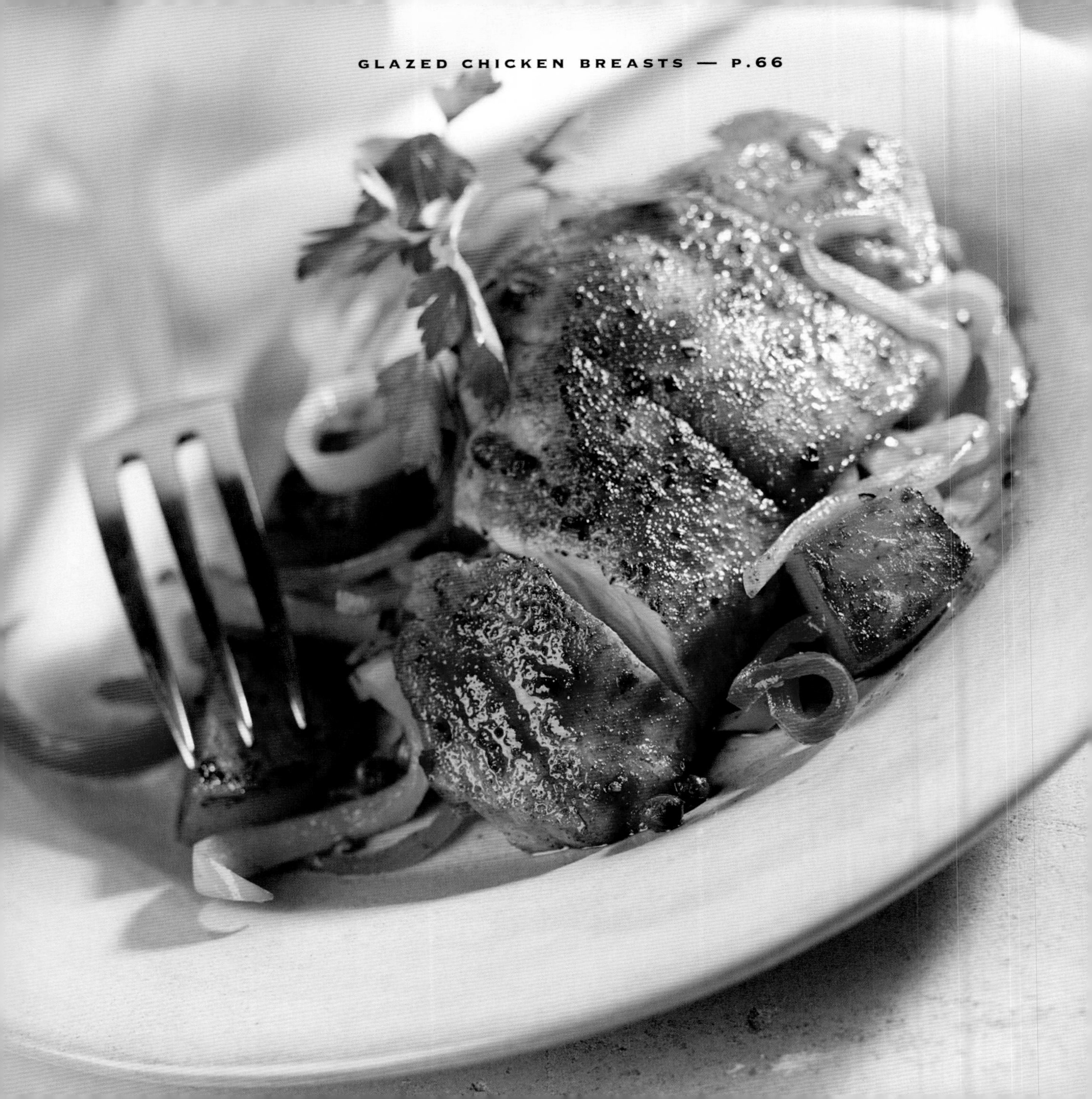

GLAZED CHICKEN BREASTS — P.66

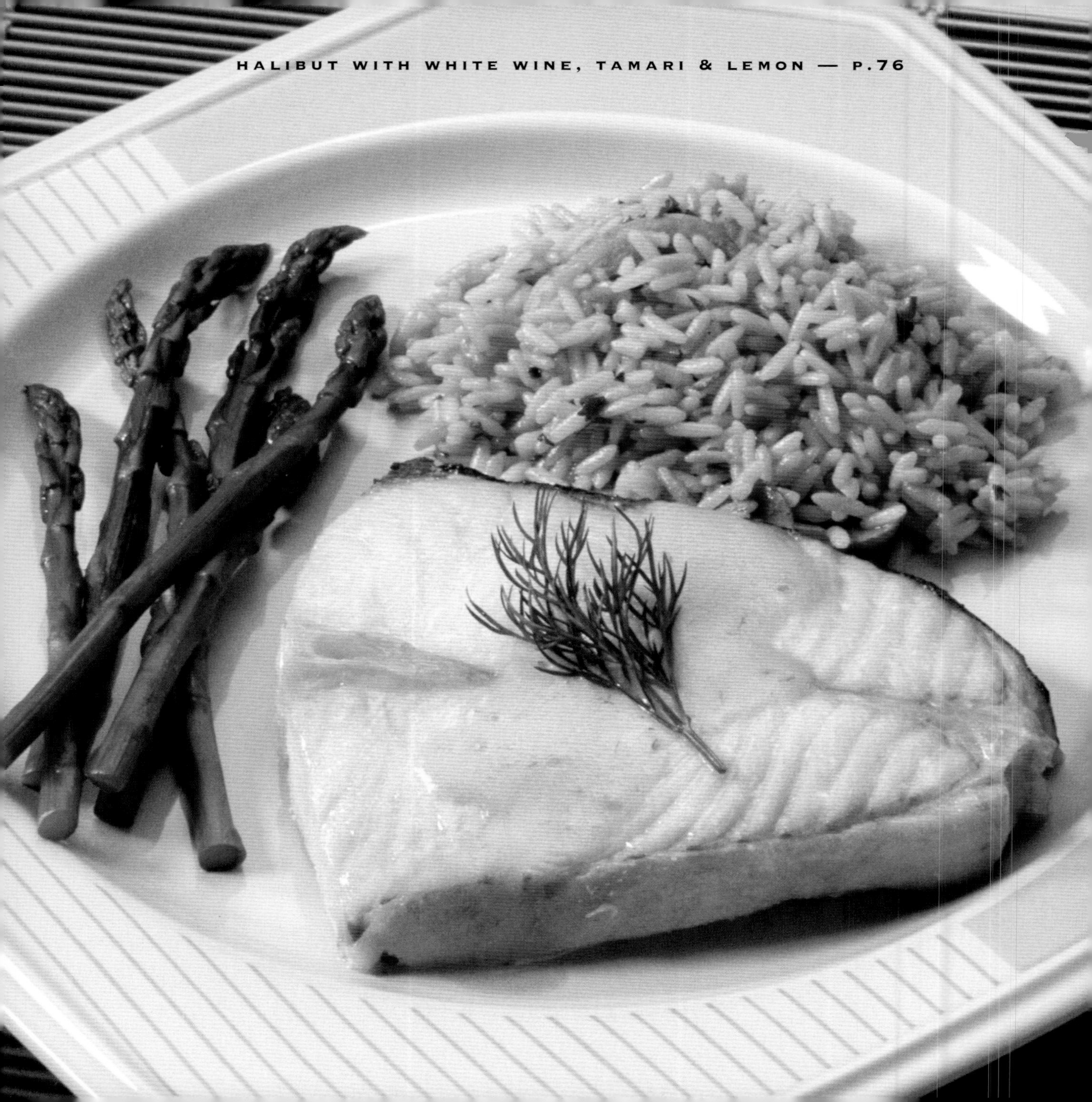

HALIBUT WITH WHITE WINE, TAMARI & LEMON — P.76

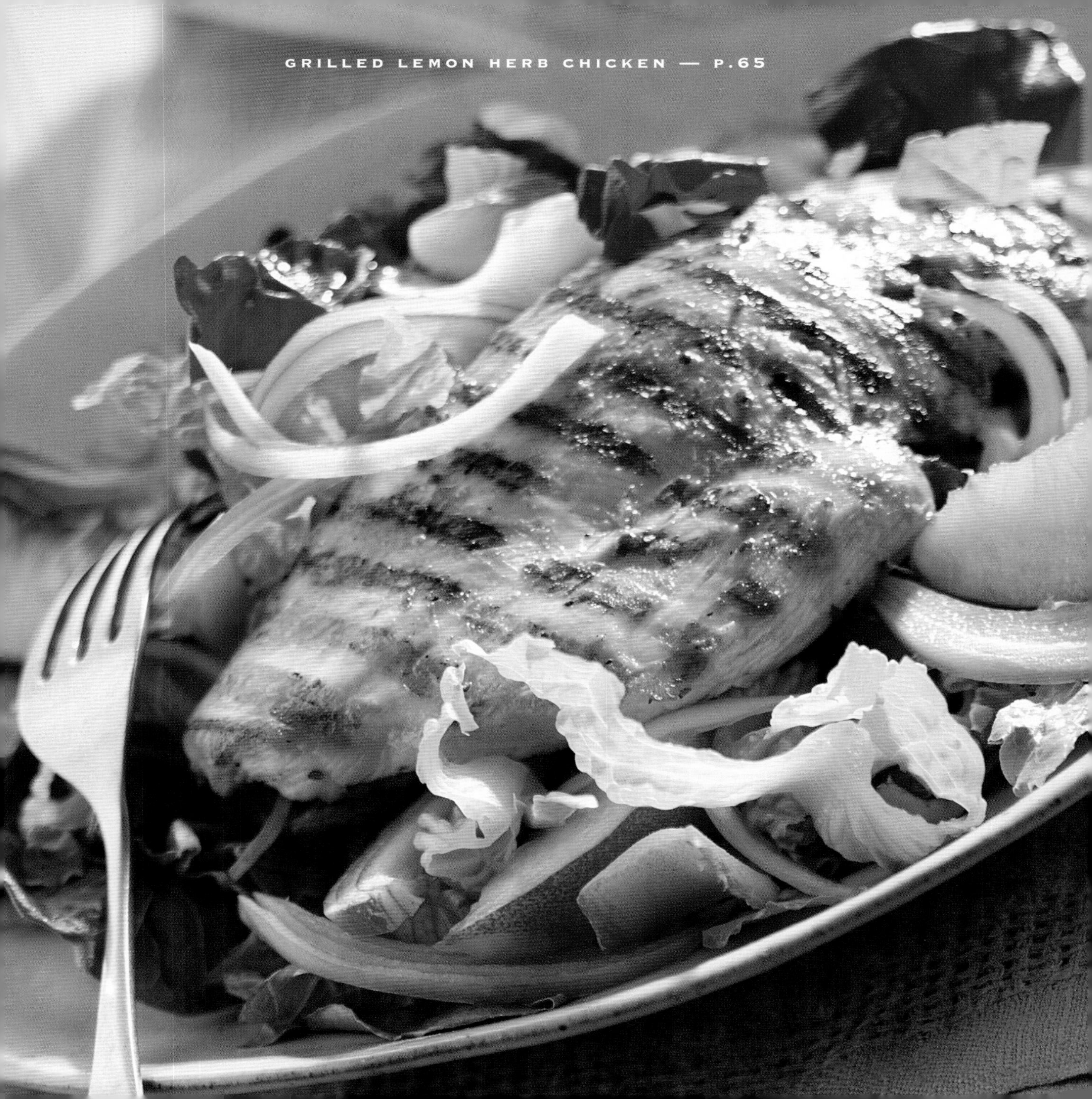

GRILLED LEMON HERB CHICKEN — P.65

Enjoy San-J's gourmet Asian products

Layered Japanese Rice Vermicelli

Rice vermicelli is delicate and light in texture. It makes the perfect accompaniment to almost any meat and vegetable combination. Look for rice vermicelli in the specialty aisle of your grocery store or in any Asian market.

Ingredients

1 1/2 pounds	pork roast
1 teaspoon	salt
1/2 teaspoon	black pepper
1 cup	fresh green cabbage, shredded
1/2 pound	rice vermicelli, cooked according to package directions, drained and cooled
1 large	cucumber, julienned
1 large	carrot, julienned
1/2 cup	San-J Tamari Peanut Salad Dressing
1/4 cup	unsalted, roasted peanuts, finely chopped

Place the roast on a rack in an ovenproof roasting pan. Season the roast with salt and black pepper. Cover tightly with aluminum foil and bake at 325°F for 2 hours, or until the meat shreds easily with a fork when pulled. A meat thermometer should read 160°F to 170°F when the roast is done. Remove from the oven and cool. Shred the meat and season again with the salt and pepper as desired. Set aside.

Prepare 4 individual serving bowls or plates. Layer the green cabbage evenly on each plate. Add the rice vermicelli in equal portions. Scatter the cucumber and carrot over the vermicelli and top each serving with generous amounts of the shredded pork. Drizzle each serving with 2 tablespoons of the San-J Tamari Peanut Salad Dressing. Garnish each serving with chopped peanuts.

MAKES 4 SERVINGS.

Maple Apple Chicken Breasts

A classic marriage of maple syrup and apples enhances these juicy, seared chicken breasts.

Ingredients

1/2 cup	maple syrup
1/8 cup	San-J Tamari
1/8 cup	fresh apple juice
1 teaspoon	ground coriander
6	boneless, skinless chicken breasts
	salt and pepper to taste
1 tablespoon	extra virgin olive oil
1/2 cup	white wine
1/2 cup	chicken broth
1 small	red delicious apple, cored and diced
1 tablespoon	maple syrup
1 tablespoon plus 2 teaspoons	all-purpose flour
2 tablespoons	butter

In a large glass or plastic mixing bowl, combine the maple syrup, San-J Tamari, apple juice and ground coriander. Place the chicken breasts in the mixture and turn to cover thoroughly. Wrap tightly with plastic wrap and refrigerate for at least 30 minutes or up to 2 hours.

Preheat the oven to 375°F. Remove the chicken breasts from the marinade, reserving the marinade, and pat the chicken dry. Season the chicken breasts with salt and pepper to taste. In a large, ovenproof skillet, heat the olive oil over medium-high heat. Sear the chicken breasts, about 2 minutes per side, until golden brown. Place the chicken in the oven and bake, covered, for an additional 10 minutes, until cooked through completely and the juices run clear. Remove the chicken from the oven, place the chicken breasts on a plate and allow the chicken to rest.

Deglaze the skillet with the white wine and chicken broth by briefly increasing the heat to medium-high and stirring the bits of cooked chicken and juices into the wine and broth. Add the diced apple and reserved marinade and bring to a boil. Reduce to a simmer and cook for 3 minutes. Add the maple syrup and flour and whisk together well to combine. Allow the sauce to cook and thicken for another 3 minutes, stirring occasionally to prevent burning or lumps. Add the butter and stir the sauce as the butter melts. Remove the sauce from the heat. To serve, plate each chicken breast individually and pour the sauce over the top of each portion.

MAKES 6 SERVINGS.

Crunchy Sweet and Sour Chicken

The snappy texture of deep-fried chicken creates the perfect foil for the soothing Asian sauce and tender-crisp vegetables. A family favorite!

Ingredients

2	egg yolks
2 tablespoons	cornstarch
1 teaspoon	salt
1/2 teaspoon	black pepper
4	boneless, skinless chicken breasts, cubed
	vegetable oil for deep frying
1 large	yellow onion, cut into large chunks
1 large	carrot, peeled and bias-cut into slices 1/4-inch thick
1 small	red pepper, cut into 1-inch pieces
1 small	orange pepper, cut into 1-inch pieces
16 ounce	can pineapple cubes in natural juice
1 tablespoon	cornstarch
1/2 cup	San-J Sweet & Tangy Sauce
2	celery ribs, cut into slices 1-inch thick
2	green onions, thinly sliced
4 cups	steamed white rice

Whisk together the egg yolks, 1 tablespoon of water, the cornstarch and salt and pepper until the mixture is very smooth. Heat the vegetable oil in a large wok or deep frying pan, filling the pan to at least 2 inches in depth. Toss the chicken cubes in the cornstarch mixture and deep-fry in batches until crisp and golden (about 5 minutes). Drain the chicken on paper towels.

Empty the oil from the wok or frying pan to leave a thin coating in the pan. Stir-fry the onion, carrot and peppers over high heat for 3 minutes, tossing the vegetables as they cook. Drain the pineapple cubes (reserving the juice), add to the pan and cook for 1 minute.

Mix together in a small bowl, the cornstarch and 1/4 cup of the pineapple juice to form a smooth paste. Add the San-J Sweet & Tangy Sauce and stir again until smooth. Pour the sauce into the wok and bring the sauce to a boil over medium-high heat, stirring until the mixture thickens.

Add the celery slices into the pan and simmer for 1 minute. Add the chicken pieces and cook for another minute, or until the chicken is heated through. Sprinkle with the sliced green onions and serve immediately over the white rice.

MAKES 4 SERVINGS.

Teriyaki Turkey Melt

*Adding teriyaki sauce to the turkey patties produces moist and flavorful results.
Jack cheese, avocado and tomatoes round out the delicious appeal of this entrée.*

Ingredients

1 1/4 pounds	ground turkey
3 cloves	garlic, minced
2 tablespoons	fresh cilantro, minced (optional)
1	egg, beaten
	salt and pepper to taste
4-5 tablespoons	San-J Teriyaki Sauce, divided
1 tablespoon	extra virgin olive oil
1 large	white onion, sliced into rings
1 cup	Jack or cheddar cheese, shredded
1	ripe avocado, peeled and sliced
1 medium	ripe tomato, sliced

In a medium mixing bowl, lightly combine the ground turkey, garlic, cilantro, egg, salt, pepper, and 1 tablespoon of San-J Teriyaki Sauce until just combined. Divide the mixture into four parts and make 4 patties. In two separate small bowls, reserve 2 tablespoons of San-J Teriyaki Sauce each.

In a small sauté pan, heat the olive oil over medium heat. Add the sliced onion and sauté until caramelized and soft. Set aside.

Preheat an oiled grill or skillet to medium. Add the turkey patties, cooking on each side for 6 to 8 minutes, or until the patties have no pink in the middle. Baste the patties with the reserved 2 tablespoons of San-J Teriyaki Sauce, brushing the patties every few minutes with the sauce.

Two minutes prior to removing the turkey patties from the heat, top each patty with the caramelized onion, a teaspoon of the reserved San-J Teriyaki Sauce, and 1/4 cup of the shredded cheese. Serve each portion as soon as the cheese is melted. Garnish each serving with the sliced avocado and tomato.

MAKES 4 SERVINGS.

Asian BBQ Chicken Pizza

Pizza takes on fresh, lively flavors with the addition of Asian sauces, chicken and fresh vegetables.
Double the recipe for a casual dinner party or to serve as appetizers.

Ingredients

	fresh pizza dough or pre-made 12-inch pizza crust
1/4 cup	San-J Asian BBQ Sauce
1/4 cup	ketchup
1/4 cup	hoisin sauce
1/2 pound	mozzarella cheese, shredded and divided
2	boneless, skinless chicken breasts, cooked and shredded
1/4 cup	red onion, thinly sliced
1 cup	fresh shiitake mushrooms, sliced
4	green onions, thinly sliced

Preheat the oven to 450°F. If using fresh pizza dough, roll out the pizza dough to make a 12-inch pizza crust. In a small bowl, combine the San-J Asian BBQ Sauce, ketchup and hoisin sauce. Brush the sauce thinly over the pizza dough or pre-made crust. Evenly sprinkle half of the shredded mozzarella cheese over the crust. Evenly arrange the chicken, red onion and mushrooms over the base layer of cheese. Scatter the remaining cheese over the chicken and mushrooms.

Place the pizza in the oven on a pizza stone or on a baking sheet and bake for 10 to 15 minutes. When done, the pizza crust will be crunchy and lightly browned and the cheese will be completely melted and bubbly. Remove the pizza from the oven and sprinkle with green onions. Cut the pizza into wedges using a pizza cutting wheel.

MAKES 6 SERVINGS.

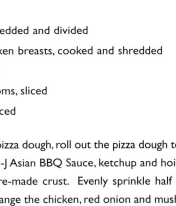

Asian BBQ Chicken Sandwich

Wasabi mayonnaise adds a unique twist to this delightful luncheon or dinner sandwich. Add condiments such as thinly sliced purple onion, avocado slices, pepper Jack cheese, etc. according to your preferences.

Ingredients

4	boneless, skinless chicken breasts
2 cups	San-J Asian BBQ Sauce
1 cup	mayonnaise
3 teaspoons	San-J Tamari
1 teaspoon	sugar
2 teaspoons	fresh lime juice
2 teaspoons	wasabi paste (you may use more or less, as desired)
4	sandwich rolls with sesame seeds, split horizontally
1 large	ripe tomato, sliced
4	iceberg lettuce leaves

Place the chicken breasts in a resealable plastic bag with the San-J Asian BBQ Sauce. Marinate at least 1 hour or up to 12 hours in the refrigerator.

Preheat an indoor or outdoor grill to medium-high heat. Place the marinated chicken breasts on the grill, and cook for about 4 or 5 minutes on each side. Cook the chicken completely until there is no pink remaining in the middle. Set aside to cool slightly.

In a small mixing bowl, whisk together the mayonnaise, San-J Tamari, sugar, lime juice and wasabi paste until smooth. To assemble, spread the wasabi mayonnaise on each side of the sandwich rolls. Place 1 chicken breast in each roll and add slices of tomato and the lettuce. Serve immediately.

MAKES 4 SERVINGS.

Grilled Lemon Herb Chicken

Fresh herbs impart a delicate flavor when added to the San-J Sweet & Tangy Sauce in this easy-to-prepare recipe.

Ingredients

1 1/2 cups	San-J Sweet & Tangy Sauce
3 tablespoons	fresh lemon juice
2 tablespoons	fresh Italian parsley, finely chopped
2 tablespoons	fresh thyme, finely chopped
2 tablespoons	fresh rosemary, finely chopped
3-4 pounds	fryer chicken, cut into individual pieces

In a large glass or plastic mixing bowl, combine the San-J Sweet & Tangy Sauce, lemon juice, parsley, thyme and rosemary. Add the chicken pieces and cover the bowl tightly with plastic wrap. Marinate the chicken in the refrigerator, turning occasionally, for at least 3 hours or overnight.

Preheat an outdoor grill to medium heat. Place the marinated chicken pieces on the grill and cook with the lid closed for 45 to 60 minutes, turning every 10 minutes. Cook until the juices run clear and a meat thermometer registers 180°F.

MAKES 6 SERVINGS.

Glazed Chicken Breasts

Simple, yet distinctive in flavor!

Ingredients

4	boneless, skinless chicken breasts
1 cup	San-J Thai Peanut Sauce, divided

Place the chicken in a resealable plastic bag with 3/4 cup of the San-J Thai Peanut Sauce. Marinate the chicken in the refrigerator for at least 1 hour or up to 12 hours.

Preheat an outdoor grill to medium-high heat. Remove the chicken from the San-J Thai Peanut Sauce and brush off any excess marinade. Discard the marinade. Place the chicken breasts on the grill and grill for 6 minutes. Turn and grill for 6 to 8 minutes, or until the chicken is cooked through completely and the juices run clear. As the chicken grills, use 1/4 cup San-J Thai Peanut Sauce as a basting sauce, liberally brushing the sauce occasionally over the chicken.

MAKES 4 SERVINGS.

Honey & Tamari Chicken

The tang of San-J Tamari meets the sweetness of honey in a delightful fusion of flavors.

Ingredients

1 cup	clover honey
1/2 cup	San-J Tamari
2 tablespoons	garlic, minced
1 tablespoon	fresh ginger, grated
4 pounds	fryer chicken, cut into individual pieces
4 cups	steamed Jasmine rice
2	green onions, thinly sliced

In a medium saucepan, combine the honey, San-J Tamari, garlic and ginger. Heat and stir over low heat until the honey is completely incorporated. Place the chicken pieces in a single layer in a large glass baking pan and pour the honey Tamari sauce over the chicken. Cover the dish tightly with plastic wrap and marinate in the refrigerator for at least 1 hour or up to 8 hours, turning the chicken occasionally.

Preheat the oven to 350°F. Place the baking pan with the chicken in the oven and bake for 1 hour, turning the chicken over after 30 minutes. Cook until the juices run clear and a meat thermometer registers 180°F. To serve, prepare 4 individual plates and spoon the rice evenly onto each plate. Top each portion of rice with the chicken pieces and spoon the remaining sauce over the chicken. Garnish the chicken with green onion slices and serve immediately.

MAKES 4 SERVINGS.

Turkey Meatballs

Meatballs simmering in a spicy San-J Asian BBQ Sauce pave the way for a substantial weekday meal.

Ingredients

2 pounds	ground turkey
1 1/2 cups	fresh white bread crumbs
1/4 cup	yellow onion, chopped
1/2 cup	San-J Asian BBQ Sauce
2	eggs, beaten
1 tablespoon	fresh Italian parsley, minced
1 1/2 cups	San-J Asian BBQ Sauce
8 ounces	hot, cooked wide egg noodles
1/4 cup	Parmesan cheese, freshly grated

Preheat the oven to 375°F. In a large mixing bowl, place the ground turkey, bread crumbs, onion, 1/2 cup San-J Asian BBQ Sauce, beaten eggs and parsley. Toss and mix thoroughly to combine. Form into meatballs, about 1 inch in size and place in a 9" x 13" glass baking pan. Bake, uncovered, for 30 minutes. Pour 1 1/2 cups of San-J Asian BBQ Sauce over the meatballs, cover, and continue baking for an additional 30 minutes. To serve, spoon the egg noodles onto a large, deep serving bowl or platter. Top the noodles with the meatballs and sauce and sprinkle the grated Parmesan cheese over all.

MAKES 8 SERVINGS.

Sweet & Tangy Baked Chicken & Winter Vegetables

The solidity of winter vegetables and chicken find perfect partnering in the San-J Sweet & Tangy Sauce.

Ingredients

4	boneless, skinless chicken breasts
I	egg, beaten
1/2 cup	cornstarch
I tablespoon	vegetable oil
2 large	carrots, peeled and sliced thinly on the diagonal
I cup	fresh green beans, washed and sliced into 1-inch pieces on the diagonal
I large	russet potato, peeled, cut in half and sliced thinly on the diagonal
I cup	San-J Sweet & Tangy Sauce

Preheat the oven to 325°F. Dip each chicken breast in the beaten egg and coat the pieces with cornstarch. In a large ovenproof sauté pan, heat the oil and saute the chicken breasts in the oil over medium-high heat until just browned, about 2 minutes on each side. Remove the sauté pan from the heat and add the carrots, green beans and potato. Pour the San-J Sweet & Tangy Sauce over the vegetables and the chicken breasts. Cover the sauté pan with a lid or aluminum foil and bake for I hour. To serve, spoon equal portions of chicken and vegetables onto individual plates.

MAKES 4 SERVINGS.

Thai-Style Chicken Pizza

This fresh approach to pizza is succulent, spicy and sure to satisfy even the toughest critic.
Be prepared for multiple requests for this recipe.

Ingredients

	fresh pizza dough or pre-made 12-inch pizza crust
1/2 cup	San-J Thai Peanut Sauce
1/2 pound	mozzarella cheese, shredded and divided
2	boneless, skinless chicken breasts, cooked and shredded
1/4 cup	red onion, thinly sliced
1 medium	carrot, julienned
1 cup	bean sprouts, cleaned
1/2 cup	roasted, salted peanuts, chopped
1/8 cup	fresh cilantro, chopped
4	green onions, thinly sliced
	dried red pepper flakes, to taste

Preheat the oven to 450°F. If using fresh pizza dough, roll out the pizza dough to make a 12-inch pizza crust. Brush the San-J Thai Peanut Sauce over the pizza dough or pre-made crust to within 1-inch of the edge of the crust. Evenly sprinkle half of the shredded mozzarella cheese over the crust. Evenly arrange the chicken and red onion over the layer of cheese, and sprinkle the remaining cheese over the chicken layer. Sprinkle the carrots and bean sprouts over the pizza and place in the oven on a pizza stone or on a baking sheet and bake for 10 to 15 minutes.

When done, the crust will be crunchy and lightly browned and the cheese will be completely melted and bubbly. Remove the pizza from the oven and sprinkle with chopped peanuts, cilantro, green onions and red pepper flakes. Cut into wedges using a pizza cutting wheel.

MAKES 6 SERVINGS.

Orange-Glazed Teriyaki Chicken Breasts

San-J Teriyaki Sauce offers a rich depth of taste and imparts a lovely grilled color.
The addition of orange brings all of that richness to completion.

Ingredients

1/2 cup	San-J Teriyaki Sauce
1 tablespoon	orange zest
1/3 cup	orange juice concentrate, thawed
2 tablespoons	fresh cilantro, minced
4	boneless, skinless chicken breasts

In a medium mixing bowl, combine the San-J Teriyaki Sauce, orange zest, orange juice and fresh cilantro. Reserve 1/4 cup of the marinade and set aside.

In a large plastic resealable bag, place the chicken breasts and add the marinade. Seal the bag and marinate in the refrigerator for at least 3 hours or up to 12 hours.

Prepare an outdoor or indoor grill at medium-high heat. Discard the used marinade. Place the chicken breasts on the grill for about 7 minutes. Baste frequently with the reserved marinade. Turn and grill again for 7 minutes, or until the juices run clear and there is no pink remaining.

MAKES 4 SERVINGS.

Tropical Swordfish & Fruit Skewers

*The combination of the swordfish and fruit brushed with the San-J Sweet & Tangy Sauce
brings delightful flavors together on the grill.*

Ingredients

2 pounds	fresh or frozen and thawed swordfish, cut into 1-inch cubes
1/2 cup	San-J Sweet & Tangy Sauce
1 cup	fresh papaya, peeled and cut into 1-inch cubes
1 cup	fresh mango, peeled and cut into 1-inch cubes
1	red onion, cut into 1-inch squares
1 large	red or yellow bell pepper, seeded and cut into 1-inch squares
12	cherry tomatoes
8	wooden skewers, soaked in water for 30 minutes
1/4 cup	San-J Sweet & Tangy Sauce

Place the swordfish cubes in a non-reactive container, such as a glass bowl. Pour the 1/2-cup of San-J Sweet & Tangy Sauce over the swordfish cubes and mix lightly to cover all of the fish with the sauce. Cover tightly with plastic wrap. Marinate the fish in the refrigerator for 2 hours. Assemble the skewers in the following order: swordfish, papaya, mango, red onion, pepper and cherry tomato.

Brush the skewers with the 1/4-cup of San-J Sweet & Tangy Sauce. Prepare an indoor or outdoor grill to high heat. Lightly oil the grids of the barbecue or fish rack prior to grilling. Grill the skewers over high heat for about 2 minutes on each side, or until the fish flakes easily with a fork and is cooked through.

MAKES 4 SERVINGS.

Maguro Butsu (MARINATED TUNA TARTARE)

Tuna tartare is sophisticated and requires very fresh fish and gentle handling.
The result is a confluence of exceptional flavors.

Ingredients

I pound	very fresh sashimi-grade tuna (ahi or yellowtail), skinned
I tablespoon	wasabi paste
5 tablespoons	San-J Tamari
6	spring onions, very thinly sliced
6	shiso leaves, cut in a chiffonade

Carefully cut the tuna into small cubes about 1/2-inch square. In a medium glass or other non-reactive bowl, combine the wasabi, San-J Tamari and onions. Add the cubed tuna and mix lightly. Cover the bowl tightly with plastic wrap. Marinate in the refrigerator for 30 minutes. Remove the tuna from the marinade and toss with the shiso ribbons. Serve immediately.

MAKES 4 SERVINGS.

Broiled Salmon with Spinach

*Purely Japanese at heart, a delicate sake broth balances the rich flavor of the salmon.
Add other seasonal vegetables to the broth as a variation.*

Marinade Ingredients

1/4 cup	San-J Tamari
3 tablespoons	sugar
2 tablespoons	mirin
2 tablespoons	sake
1 teaspoon	fresh ginger, grated
1 clove	garlic, minced
4	7 ounce salmon fillets
	salt and pepper to taste

Broth Ingredients

2 cups	chicken broth
1 tablespoon	San-J Tamari
2 teaspoons	mirin
2 teaspoons	rice vinegar
1 clove	garlic, minced
1 teaspoon	fresh ginger, grated
1 teaspoon	sugar
1/2 teaspoon	toasted sesame oil
6 cups	fresh spinach leaves, cleaned and lightly packed

Prepare the marinade in a mixing bowl by combining the San-J Tamari, sugar, mirin, sake, ginger and garlic. Whisk to mix well. Place the salmon fillets in a glass pan (or other non-reactive pan) and pour the marinade over the top. Cover tightly with plastic wrap and refrigerate at least 2 hours or up to 4 hours.

Preheat the broiler to high heat. Remove the salmon fillets from the marinade and pat dry. In a saucepan, heat the marinade to boiling and cook for 5 minutes. Season each fillet with salt and pepper to taste. Place the fillets on the broiler pan and broil for 6 to 7 minutes. Baste every 2 minutes with the marinade. Turn and continue broiling for 6 to 7 minutes. Set aside and keep warm.

In a large stockpot or saucepan, combine the chicken broth, San-J Tamari, mirin, rice vinegar, garlic, ginger, sugar, and sesame oil and bring to a boil. Simmer for 5 minutes, stirring occasionally. Add the spinach leaves, covering the spinach with the broth and continue simmering for 30 seconds. To serve, ladle the broth and spinach into 4 shallow bowls and place a broiled salmon fillet on top of each serving.

MAKES 4 SERVINGS.

Halibut with White Wine, Tamari & Lemon

A remarkably light entrée that brings full flavor to the table.

Ingredients

1/4 cup	San-J Tamari
1/4 cup	dry white wine
4 tablespoons	extra virgin olive oil
2 tablespoons	fresh lemon juice
2 cloves	garlic, thinly sliced
4	7 ounce fresh halibut fillets
	salt and pepper to taste
2 large	zucchini, washed and thinly sliced
6 large	shiitake mushrooms, stems removed, sliced
	extra-heavy duty aluminum foil

In a large glass or other non-reactive bowl, combine the San-J Tamari, wine, olive oil, lemon juice and garlic. Place the halibut fillets in the bowl and spoon the Tamari marinade over the fillets. Cover tightly with plastic wrap and marinate in the refrigerator for 30 minutes. Remove the halibut from the marinade and season both sides of each fillet with salt and pepper to taste. Reserve the marinade.

Preheat the oven to 450°F. Cut four large sheets of aluminum foil, each about 12" x 16" in size. On the center of each piece of foil, place equal portions of the zucchini and mushroom slices. Place a seasoned halibut fillet on top of each serving of vegetables, and bring up the sides of the foil to form a pouch with a small opening in the top. Through the opening in the top of each pouch, pour one-fourth of the reserved marinade on the halibut fillet. Seal the foil so that no liquid or steam can escape.

Place the sealed foil pouches on a baking sheet and bake in the oven for 20 to 30 minutes. Test the fish in one pouch by opening the foil carefully (hot steam will escape) and flaking the fish with a fork. It will flake easily when the fish is cooked. To serve, unwrap each pouch and place each fillet in a shallow bowl. Pour the vegetables and broth over each fillet.

MAKES 4 SERVINGS.

Pan-Seared Ahi Tuna Steaks

To ensure excellent results, use only the freshest ahi tuna. The dipping sauce adds a special touch of interest.

Tuna Steak Ingredients

4	8 ounce fresh tuna steaks, cut about 1-inch thick
2 tablespoons	vegetable oil, divided
	salt and pepper to taste
1 cup	untoasted sesame seeds

Tamari-Ginger Sauce Ingredients

1/4 cup	San-J Tamari
1/8 cup	rice wine vinegar
1/8 cup	fresh lime juice
3 tablespoons	sugar
2	green onions, thinly sliced
2 teaspoons	fresh ginger, minced
1 teaspoon	toasted sesame oil
1/2 teaspoon	dried red pepper flakes

Pat the tuna steaks very dry using paper towels. Rub both sides of each steak with 1 tablespoon of the vegetable oil and season with salt and pepper. Pour the sesame seeds onto a shallow plate or dish. Coat each side of the steaks with the sesame seeds by pressing the fish into the seeds.

Heat 1 tablespoon of the vegetable oil in a nonstick sauté pan over high heat until the oil is very hot and just about to smoke. Add the tuna steaks and sear for 45 seconds without moving the steaks. Reduce the heat to medium and continue to cook for another 1 1/2 minutes. Flip the steaks over and cook for another 2 minutes for rare tuna steaks, or 3 minutes for medium-rare. Cut the steaks on the diagonal into 1/4-inch slices. Plate the tuna steak slices on a platter lined with lettuce leaves.

Prepare the dipping sauce by whisking together in a small bowl the San-J Tamari, vinegar, lime juice, sugar, green onion, ginger, sesame oil and red pepper flakes. Whisk vigorously to blend. Serve immediately with the tuna steaks.

MAKES 4 SERVINGS.

Ginger Halibut in Cabbage Leaves

Sweet ginger and honey contrast beautifully with the San-J Sweet & Tangy Sauce in this delightful entrée.

Ingredients

1 1/2 pounds	halibut fillets or steaks
2 tablespoons	San-J Sweet & Tangy Sauce
12	napa cabbage leaves
1 tablespoon	vegetable oil
2 cloves	garlic, minced
2 tablespoons	ginger, minced
1/4 cup	shallots, minced
1	red bell pepper, seeded and finely chopped
1 tablespoon	fresh mint, minced
1 tablespoon	fresh cilantro, minced

Citrus Sauce Ingredients

1 tablespoon	honey
1 tablespoon	San-J Sweet & Tangy Sauce
4 tablespoons	orange juice
1 tablespoon	lemon juice

Cut the halibut into cubes about 1/2-inch in size, place in a glass bowl and add 2 tablespoons of the San-J Sweet & Tangy Sauce. Cover tightly with plastic wrap and marinate in the refrigerator for at least 30 minutes or up to 2 hours.

Bring a large pot of salted water to a boil and blanch the cabbage leaves by dipping them into the water until the leaves are soft and pliable, about 3 minutes. Set the drained cabbage leaves aside. In a medium sauté pan, heat the vegetable oil on medium heat and sauté the garlic, ginger, shallots and red pepper until they are soft, about 4 minutes. Toss lightly as the vegetables sauté. Remove the vegetables from the heat and add the fish cubes, mint and cilantro. Toss lightly again to combine thoroughly.

Place two cabbage leaves on a flat work surface, overlapping slightly, to make 6 sets of 2 leaves each. Divide the fish and vegetables evenly among the 6 sets of cabbage leaves. Roll the cabbage leaves, tucking in the sides, to form an enclosed roll, and secure with toothpicks. Steam the cabbage rolls for 9 minutes, or until cooked through. To test, unwrap one roll and flake the fish with a fork. It should flake easily when ready to serve.

Prepare the sauce as the cabbage rolls steam by combining the honey, San-J Sweet & Tangy Sauce, orange juice and lemon juice in a small saucepan. Whisk and heat over medium until the honey is smooth and the sauce is warm. To serve, drizzle the thickened sauce over each cooked halibut roll.

MAKES 6 SERVINGS.

Szechuan Prawns

Prawns and white wine with a touch of San-J Szechuan Sauce combine to make a dazzling entrée that is at once elementary and refined. Add the fresh Italian parsley for a bright splash of color.

Ingredients

2 pounds	fresh prawns, peeled, deveined, tails on
1/2 cup	San-J Szechuan Sauce
1 tablespoon	extra virgin olive oil
3 cloves	garlic, minced
1/4 cup	dry white wine
2 tablespoons	butter or margarine
1 tablespoon	fresh Italian parsley, chopped
8 cups	steamed white rice

In a large glass or other non-reactive bowl, place the prawns and San-J Szechuan Sauce. Mix well and cover tightly. Marinate in the refrigerator for 30 minutes.

In a large skillet, heat the olive oil on medium heat. Add the garlic and cook for 1 minute. Add the marinated prawns, the marinade and white wine. Bring to a boil, then reduce the heat to simmer for 4 minutes. Add the butter and blend with a spoon to melt. Remove the prawns from the heat and stir in the parsley. Serve immediately, spooning the prawns and sauce over the steamed rice.

MAKES 6 SERVINGS.

❋

Cracked Pepper Salmon

The robust nature of grilled salmon carries the garlic and chive butter with ease.

Ingredients

4	6 ounce salmon fillets
1 cup	San-J Cracked Pepper Sauce
1 whole	head of garlic
2 tablespoons	extra virgin olive oil
1/4 cup	unsalted butter
3 tablespoons	fresh chives, minced
1/2 teaspoon	salt

Place the salmon fillets in a 9" x 13" glass pan and add the San-J Cracked Pepper Sauce. Turn to coat the fish with the sauce. Cover the pan tightly with plastic wrap and marinate in the refrigerator at least 1 hour or up to 12 hours.

Preheat the oven to 400°F. Cut off the top of the head of garlic to expose the garlic flesh underneath the paper skins. Place the garlic head in a large square of aluminum foil and drizzle with the olive oil. Sprinkle with salt to taste. Crumple up the aluminum foil to create an airtight pocket and bake for 45 minutes, or until the garlic is very soft and roasted. Remove the garlic from the oven and cool.

In a small food processor or in a mixing bowl, mix together 5 cloves of the roasted garlic, the butter, chives and salt. Blend until the butter is very smooth. Place in the refrigerator.

Preheat an outdoor grill to medium-high heat. Lightly oil the barbecue grids. Grill the salmon fillets for 4 minutes. Turn and grill for 4 minutes. Remove the salmon when it is cooked through, but not dry or flaking. Top each fillet with a dollop of the roasted garlic-chive butter. Serve immediately.

MAKES 4 SERVINGS.

Carmelized Salmon Teriyaki

Beautifully glazed salmon fillets are the masterpiece of any special meal.

Ingredients

4	5 to 7 ounce salmon fillets
1/2 cup	San-J Teriyaki Sauce
1 tablespoon	sugar

Place the salmon fillets in a shallow glass or other non-reactive bowl and pour the San-J Teriyaki Sauce over the fillets. Spoon the sauce and turn the fillets to coat each with the sauce. Cover tightly with plastic wrap and marinate in the refrigerator for at least 30 minutes or up to 4 hours.

Preheat an indoor or outdoor grill to medium heat. Lightly oil the grids of the grill. Remove the salmon from the marinade and pat each fillet dry with paper towels. Reserve the marinade.

To prepare the sauce, pour the reserved marinade into a small saucepan and add the sugar. Heat and stir over medium-high heat until the sugar has dissolved and the San-J Teriyaki Sauce has thickened.

Grill the salmon for about 4 minutes. Baste the salmon with the marinade sauce as it grills. Turn each fillet and grill for 4 minutes, basting again with sauce and watching carefully to avoid overcooking the fish. The marinade sauce will lightly caramelize as the fillets grill.

MAKES 4 SERVINGS.

Cracked Peppercorn Spareribs

Piquant and well-seasoned, these pork spareribs reap the benefits of both a dry spice rub and San-J's delicious Cracked Pepper Sauce.

Ingredients

4 pounds	pork spareribs
1 teaspoon	salt
1 teaspoon	black pepper
1 teaspoon	chili powder
2 cups	San-J Cracked Pepper Sauce, plus additional sauce for basting

Cut the ribs into serving pieces and place in a large glass baking dish. Combine the salt, pepper and chili powder and rub the spices all over the spareribs. Let the ribs stand for 30 minutes. Preheat the oven to 375°F. Pour the San-J Cracked Pepper Sauce over the ribs, turning the ribs to coat. Bake for 1 hour, basting and turning the ribs every 15 minutes.

MAKES 6 SERVINGS.

Asian BBQ Sirloin Steak

Colorful and richly basted with sauce, this sirloin steak over rice is an elegant offering.

Ingredients

1 teaspoon	extra virgin olive oil
1 large	yellow onion, finely chopped
1	green bell pepper, seeded and finely chopped
1 clove	garlic, minced
1 1/2 pounds	sirloin steak, fat removed and thinly sliced
1 cup	San-J Asian BBQ Sauce
1 large	ripe tomato, cut into eighths
8 cups	steamed white rice

In a large skillet or sauté pan, heat the olive oil over medium-high heat. Add the onion, pepper and garlic, and sauté until soft and the onion is translucent, about 3 minutes. Add the sirloin steak slices and cook until browned. Drain off any excess liquid. Add the San-J Asian BBQ Sauce and bring to a boil. Reduce the heat and simmer for 30 minutes. Add the tomato and simmer for 2 minutes. Serve over the steamed rice.

MAKES 6 SERVINGS.

Broccoli Beef

A fusion of Japanese and American cooking that has become a popular entrée.
The San-J Cracked Pepper Sauce used in this recipe adds a delicious complement to the beef.

Ingredients

1/4 cup	all-purpose flour
10 ounce	can low-sodium beef broth
2 tablespoons	San-J Cracked Pepper Sauce
1 1/2 tablespoons	honey
1 tablespoon	vegetable oil
1 teaspoon	fresh ginger, minced
2 cloves	garlic, minced
1 pound	boneless round steak, cut into bite-sized slices
2	red bell peppers, seeded and cut into thin strips
4 cups	broccoli florets
6 cups	steamed white rice

In a medium mixing bowl, combine the flour, broth, San-J Cracked Pepper Sauce and honey, whisking to blend thoroughly. In a large sauté pan, heat the oil and add the ginger, garlic and steak. Heat and stir on medium-high heat for about 4 minutes. Add the broth mixture, red pepper strips, and broccoli florets. Bring the beef and vegetables to a boil and simmer for 8 minutes until beef is cooked through. Serve over the rice.

MAKES 4 SERVINGS.

Savory Elegant Meatloaf

Transformed by fresh thyme and San-J Tamari, this meatloaf is appropriate for a casual dinner with friends.

Ingredients

2 large	yellow onions, finely chopped
2 tablespoons	extra virgin olive oil
2 teaspoons	kosher salt
1 teaspoon	freshly ground black pepper
1 teaspoon	fresh thyme leaves, minced (you may substitute 1/2 teaspoon dried thyme)
3 cloves	garlic, minced
1/3 cup	San-J Tamari
3/4 cup	beef or chicken broth
1 1/2 teaspoons	tomato paste
5 pounds	lean ground beef
1 1/2 cups	plain bread crumbs
3 extra-large	eggs, beaten
1 teaspoon	fresh parsley, minced (you may substitute 1/2 teaspoon dried parsley)
3/4 cup	ketchup

In a medium sauté pan, cook the onions, olive oil, salt, pepper and thyme over medium-low heat until the onions are translucent, but not browned, approximately 15 minutes. About 2 minutes before the onions are completely cooked, add the minced garlic and stir to combine. Add the San-J Tamari, broth and tomato paste and mix well. Remove the onions from the heat and allow the onions to cool to room temperature.

Preheat the oven to 325°F. Combine the ground beef, bread crumbs, eggs, parsley and onion mixture in a large bowl. Toss and mix until just combined and shape into a rectangular loaf. Place the loaf in an ungreased rectangular 9" x 13" glass or metal pan. Spread the ketchup evenly over the top of the meatloaf and bake for 1 1/2 hours, or until the internal temperature is 160°F when tested with a meat thermometer. Remove the meatloaf from oven and let stand for 5 minutes. Slice into portions about 1/2-inch thick and serve immediately.

MAKES 8 SERVINGS.

Asian-Style Beef Stroganoff

East meets West in this beautiful fusion of Eastern European sour cream and beef combined with mushrooms and San-J Tamari.

Ingredients

2 tablespoons	extra virgin olive oil
4	5 to 6 ounce filet mignon pieces, cut crosswise into pieces 1/4-inch thick
2 tablespoons	unsalted butter
1 1/2 cups	yellow onion, finely chopped
	salt and pepper to taste
1/2 pound	fresh shiitake mushrooms, stems discarded and caps thinly sliced
1/2 pound	oyster mushrooms
2 tablespoons	all-purpose flour
1 cup	dry sake
1 1/2 cups	beef broth
1/2 cup	dairy sour cream
1 tablespoon	San-J Tamari, or to taste
1/4 cup	fresh cilantro leaves, finely chopped
1 package	fresh Chinese or dried American egg noodles, cooked and drained

In a large sauté pan, heat the olive oil over moderately high heat and brown the beef in small batches, transferring the beef to a plate with a slotted spoon or tongs.

Add the butter to the sauté pan and cook the onions over moderate heat, seasoning them with salt and pepper to taste. Stir and sauté until the onions are softened. Add all of the mushrooms and cook, stirring, until tender. Sprinkle the flour over the vegetables and blend again, stirring 1 minute. Add the sake and bring the sauce to a boil. Reduce the heat and simmer until almost all of the liquid has evaporated Add the beef broth and simmer 1 minute. Stir in the sour cream and San-J Tamari, blending gently over low heat.

Return the beef to the skillet and gently simmer, carefully stirring occasionally, until the beef is warmed through, about 3 to 5 minutes. Do not allow the sauce to boil or break down the sour cream due to heat. Add the cilantro and adjust the sauce with salt and pepper as needed. Arrange the noodles on a large serving platter and spoon the beef and sauce over the noodles.

MAKES 4 SERVINGS.

Seared Steak with Caramelized Onions

Who can resist a perfectly grilled steak? The caramelized onions add a hint of sweetness.
Serve this entrée with pomme frites as a French accompaniment.

Ingredients

4	8 ounce sirloin steaks
4 tablespoons	San-J Cracked Pepper Sauce
I tablespoon	extra virgin olive oil
2 large	yellow onions, thinly sliced
I teaspoon	fresh thyme, minced
1/2 teaspoon	salt
1/4 teaspoon	black pepper

Place the steaks in a shallow glass pan and pour the San-J Cracked Pepper Sauce over all. Turn the steaks to coat thoroughly. Cover the pan tightly with plastic wrap and marinate in the refrigerator for at least 30 minutes or up to 4 hours.

As the steaks marinate, prepare the caramelized onion topping. Heat the olive oil in a large sauté pan over medium-high heat. Add the onion slices, thyme and remaining seasonings and stir to blend. After 2 minutes, reduce the heat to medium-low and allow the onions to cook as they slowly release their natural sweetness. When done, the onions should be slightly browned, but not black.

Prepare an indoor or outdoor grill on high heat. Remove the steaks from the marinade and pat them dry with paper towels. Season each steak with salt and pepper to taste. Sear I side of each steak on high heat for about 2 minutes. Turn and sear the other side of each steak for 2 minutes. Lower the grill heat to medium or, as an alternative, place the steaks in a 400°F oven and cook to your preferred doneness. To serve, place each steak on an individual plate and surround with the caramelized onion. Pass additional San-J Cracked Pepper Sauce at the table, if desired.

MAKES 4 SERVINGS.

Steak & Red Pepper Kabobs

Japanese steak sauce is unique-it carries deep soy flavor along with the more traditional steak flavoring. This entrée basks in the flavor of the San-J Japanese Steak Sauce.

Ingredients

1 1/2 pounds	boneless beef sirloin steak, cut into 1 1/2-inch cubes
3 cloves	garlic, minced
1 cup	San-J Japanese Steak Sauce, divided, plus additional sauce for basting
1 cup	zucchini, cut into 1/2-inch slices
1 cup	red bell pepper, cut into large bite-sized pieces
1 cup	yellow onion, cut into large bite-sized pieces
8	bamboo skewers, soaked in water for at least 30 minutes

In a medium mixing bowl, combine the steak cubes, garlic and 1/2 cup of the San-J Japanese Steak Sauce. Cover tightly with plastic wrap and marinate in the refrigerator at least 1 hour or overnight. In a large mixing bowl, combine the vegetables and 1/2 cup of the San-J Japanese Steak Sauce. Cover tightly with plastic wrap and marinate at room temperature for 30 minutes.

Assemble the skewers by alternating the beef and vegetables evenly on each of the skewers. Prepare a grill on medium-high heat. Grill the skewers for 5 minutes. Baste and turn each skewer. Grill for 5 minutes and baste again. Turn again and baste, grilling for 3 to 5 minutes, or until the meat is cooked through.

MAKES 4 SERVINGS.

Lamb Pita Sandwiches

Although lamb is not typically paired with steak sauce, you'll find these pockets of seasoned lamb, feta cheese and vegetables to be a delightful change of pace.

Ingredients

2 pounds	ground lamb
1 cup	plain bread crumbs
1	egg, beaten
1/2 cup	San-J Japanese Steak Sauce, divided
1/4 cup	yellow onion, chopped
8 ounces	feta cheese, sliced
2 large	ripe tomatoes, sliced
1/2 head	iceberg lettuce, shredded
14 ounce	can Greek kalamata olives, pitted
1 cup	plain yogurt
8 whole	pieces of pita bread, cut into halves
2	lemons, cut into wedges

Preheat the oven to 375°F. In a large bowl, combine the lamb, bread crumbs, egg, 1/4 cup of the San-J Japanese Steak Sauce and the onion. Shape into meatballs, about 1-inch in size. Place the meatballs in a 9" x 13" glass baking pan and bake, uncovered, for 30 minutes. Drizzle the meatballs with 1/4 cup of the San-J Japanese Steak Sauce and bake for another 20 minutes.

Place the feta cheese, tomatoes, lettuce and kalamata olives on a serving dish. You or your guests can assemble the pita sandwiches by stuffing each pita half with 2 or 3 meatballs. Add the feta cheese, tomatoes, lettuce and kalamata olives. Drizzle each pita sandwich with plain yogurt and a squeeze of lemon.

MAKES 8 SERVINGS.

Honey Marinated Flank Steak

The sweetness of the honey adds a delightful twist to this grilled steak. Slice the steak very thinly to serve.

Ingredients

1 cup	San-J Japanese Steak Sauce
1/4 cup	clover honey
1 1/2 pounds	flank steak

In a small mixing bowl, whisk together the San-J Japanese Steak Sauce and honey until well combined. Place flank steak in a large plastic, resealable bag and pour the marinade over the steak, turning to coat the steak completely. Marinate the steak in the refrigerator at least 8 hours or up to 12 hours, turning the bag over frequently to coat each side of the steak.

Prepare an indoor or outdoor grill to medium-high heat. Grill the steak for 8 to 10 minutes. Turn and grill for 8 minutes. Test the steak for doneness (some pink should remain in the center), or grill until cooked to your preference. Remove the steak to a large carving board and let stand for 5 minutes. Slice the steak very thinly against the grain of the meat and place the slices on a large serving platter.

MAKES 6 SERVINGS.

Tonkatsu (PANKO-BREADED PORK CUTLETS)

A traditional Japanese entrée that is at once both crunchy and savory.
Serve with steamed white rice and shredded cabbage.

Ingredients

	vegetable oil for deep-frying
4	6 ounce pork cutlets, deboned
1 cup	all-purpose flour
1/2 teaspoon	salt
1/2 teaspoon	freshly ground black pepper
2	eggs, beaten
1 1/2 cups	panko breadcrumbs
1 cup	San-J Japanese Steak Sauce
1/2 cup	ketchup
1 whole	white cabbage, thinly shredded
6 cups	steamed white rice

Pour about 3 inches of vegetable oil into a deep fryer or large saucepan and heat to 350°F.

Make a few deep cuts horizontally across the grain of the pork to prevent it from curling up as it cooks. In a shallow dish, combine the flour, salt and pepper. In another shallow dish, place the beaten eggs. Place the panko breadcrumbs in another shallow dish. Dip the meat into the flour and shake off the excess. Dip the floured meat into the beaten egg and then coat with the breadcrumbs. Deep-fry each pork cutlet for 8 to 10 minutes, until golden brown. Place on a rack or paper towels to drain.

In a small bowl, combine the San-J Japanese Steak Sauce and the ketchup. To serve, place even portions of the cabbage on 4 individual plates. Top each with a pork cutlet. Spoon the sauce over each cutlet. Serve the rice on the side.

MAKES 4 SERVINGS.

Grilled Bourbon Steak

Blend bourbon with San-J Cracked Pepper Sauce and the results are juicy and succulent steaks grilled to perfection.

Ingredients

1 cup	bourbon
2 cups	San-J Cracked Pepper Sauce
2 tablespoons	honey
2 cloves	garlic, minced
3 pounds	top sirloin steak

In a large mixing bowl, whisk together the bourbon, San-J Cracked Pepper Sauce, honey and garlic. Place the steak in a large resealable plastic bag and add the bourbon sauce. Seal the bag and marinate the steak in the refrigerator for at least 1 hour or up to 5 hours, turning the bag every 30 minutes.

Preheat a grill to medium-high heat. Place the steak on the grill and cook as desired. The length of grilling time will be determined by the thickness of your steak. A meat thermometer will register 165°F when the meat is medium with some pink remaining. After grilling, remove the steak to a carving board and let stand for 5 minutes. Slice the steak thinly against the grain and serve immediately.

MAKES 6 SERVINGS.

Spicy Pork and Tofu Stir-Fry

Colorful vegetables are stir-fried quickly to a crisp perfection.
The addition of pork and the San-J Cracked Pepper Sauce create a memorable entrée.

Ingredients

1 pound	pork tenderloin, cubed
1 cup	San-J Cracked Pepper Sauce, divided
14 ounce	container firm tofu, drained and cubed
2 tablespoons	vegetable oil
1 tablespoon	fresh ginger, grated
1	fresh green chile, seeded and minced
1/2 cup	carrots, julienned
1/2 cup	chicken broth
1 teaspoon	cornstarch
1/2 cup	sugar snap peas, trimmed
1/2 cup	broccoli florets
8 cups	steamed white rice
4	green onions, thinly sliced

Place the cubed pork in a medium bowl. Add 1/2 cup of the San-J Cracked Pepper Sauce and cover tightly with plastic wrap. Marinate in the refrigerator for 1 hour. In a separate bowl, marinate the tofu cubes in 1/2 cup San-J Cracked Pepper Sauce for at least 30 minutes.

In a large skillet or wok, heat the vegetable oil on medium-high heat. Stir in the ginger and chile pepper for 1 minute. Remove the pork and tofu from the marinades and place in the wok. Add 2 tablespoons of the marinade from the tofu. Add the carrots and stir to combine. Stir-fry for 5 minutes, or until the pork is tender. Add the chicken broth and cornstarch and simmer for another 4 minutes until the sauce thickens. Add the sugar snap peas and broccoli and simmer for another 3 minutes. Serve over the rice and garnish with the green onions.

MAKES 6 SERVINGS.

Tangy Pork Chops with Sweet Corn Relish

A subtle apple flavor highlights the deliciously sweet corn relish and juicy pork chops.

Ingredients

1 tablespoon	extra virgin olive oil
6	6 ounce pork loin chops
	salt and pepper to taste
1 large	white onion, finely chopped
1 cup	San-J Sweet & Tangy Sauce
1 cup	apple juice
1/2 cup	chicken broth
1 1/2 cups	frozen kernel corn, thawed

In a large skillet, heat the oil on medium-high heat until hot, but not smoking. Season each side of the pork loin chops with salt and pepper. Sauté the onions for 1 minute and then add the pork loin chops, browning them on both sides, about 2 minutes each.

In a medium mixing bowl, combine the San-J Sweet & Tangy Sauce, apple juice and chicken broth and blend well. Add the sauce to the pork chops and bring the sauce to a boil. Reduce the heat and simmer for 20 minutes, or until the chops are cooked through. About 3 minutes before the chops are done, add the corn. To serve, place the chops on a large platter and spoon the corn, onions and sauce over the chops.

MAKES 6 SERVINGS.

Tamari Mustard Pork Tenderloin

A provocative mustard marinade brings out the best of the pork tenderloin.

Ingredients

2 pounds	pork tenderloin
1/4 cup	honey mustard
1 cup	San-J Tamari Mustard Salad Dressing

Coat the pork tenderloin with the honey mustard and place in a large mixing bowl. Pour the San-J Tamari Mustard Salad Dressing over the pork tenderloin and cover tightly with plastic wrap. Marinate the pork in the refrigerator for at least 6 hours or up to 12 hours. Turn the tenderloin over several times to marinate each side.

Preheat the oven to 350°F. Remove the tenderloin from the marinade and wrap the tenderloin in aluminum foil, securing the ends tightly so that no steam can escape. Bake for 1 1/2 hours or until a meat thermometer reaches 170°F. Remove the tenderloin from the foil and allow it to stand for 10 minutes. Carve the tenderloin into slices about 1/4-inch thick.

MAKES 8 SERVINGS.

Asian BBQ Beef

A perfect entrée for a warm evening or an excellent choice as a starter course.

Ingredients

1 1/2 pounds	boneless beef sirloin, sliced into 1/4-inch strips
1 1/2 cups	San-J Asian BBQ Sauce
6 cloves	garlic, minced
3 tablespoons	fresh ginger, grated
8	green onions, thinly sliced
1 tablespoon	sugar
1 tablespoon	Asian chile oil
1 tablespoon	toasted sesame oil
2 tablespoons	sesame seeds
1/8 cup	fresh cilantro, minced
6 servings	steamed white rice

Place the steak in a rectangular glass pan. In a medium mixing bowl, combine the San-J Asian BBQ Sauce, garlic, ginger, green onions, sugar, chile oil, sesame oil, sesame seeds and cilantro and mix thoroughly to combine. Pour the marinade over the steak and cover tightly with plastic wrap. Marinate in the refrigerator for at least 3 hours or up to 8 hours.

Heat a grill on high heat. Once the grill is very hot, remove the beef strips from the marinade and place them on the grill, cooking about 2 minutes per side or until cooked through. Serve over white rice.

MAKES 6 SERVINGS.

Barbecued Asian Spareribs

Quick and easy preparation with stellar results!

Ingredients

1 1/2 cups	San-J Asian BBQ Sauce
2 pounds	pork spareribs
2	green onions, thinly sliced

In a large mixing bowl, pour the San-J Asian BBQ Sauce over the pork spareribs. Turn the ribs to coat thoroughly. Cover tightly with plastic wrap and marinate in the refrigerator for 4 to 6 hours.

Preheat the oven to 350°F. Remove the spareribs from the marinade and dry off any excess marinade with paper towels. In a saucepan, heat the marinade to boiling and cook for 5 minutes. Place the spareribs on a rack in a shallow roasting pan and place the pan in the oven for 45 minutes, basting with the reserved marinade every 15 minutes. Increase the oven temperature to 400°F and bake for another 15 minutes until browned. Remove from the oven and sprinkle with green onion slices.

MAKES 4 SERVINGS.

Summer Vegetables & Pork Stir-Fry

Use any seasonal fresh vegetables in this entrée for added nutritional value. Light and delicious!

Ingredients

1 tablespoon	vegetable oil
1/2 pound	lean pork, cut into thin strips
	salt and pepper to taste
1	red bell pepper, seeded and sliced
1 clove	garlic, minced
2 cups	sugar snap peas, cleaned and trimmed
1 large	carrot, cut into 1/4-inch slices, lightly blanched
1/4 cup	dry sherry
1 cup	San-J Thai Peanut Sauce
4 cups	steamed white rice

In a large skillet or wok heat the vegetable oil over medium-high heat. As soon as the oil is hot, add the pork slices and brown them, stirring as they sauté. Cook for about 3 minutes. Season the pork with salt and pepper to taste. Add the red bell pepper and garlic and stir-fry for another minute. Add the sugar snap peas, carrot, sherry and the San-J Thai Peanut Sauce. Bring the sauce to a simmer and cook, stirring occasionally, for another 4 minutes. Serve immediately over the rice.

MAKES 4 SERVINGS.

Savory Tofu with Steamed Vegetables

This delicious combination of tofu and vegetables is a satisfying, complete meal in itself.

Ingredients

1 pound	firm tofu, drained
1 cup	San-J Thai Peanut Sauce
2 cups	fresh broccoli florets
1/2 cup	carrots, thinly sliced
1/2 cup	canned water chestnuts, thinly sliced
2	green onions, thinly sliced

Cut the tofu into bite-sized cubes and place in a large glass bowl. Pour the San-J Thai Peanut Sauce over the tofu and stir gently to combine. Cover tightly with plastic wrap and marinate at least 1 hour or up to 4 hours.

Preheat the oven to 375°F. Remove any excess marinade from the tofu and reserve the marinade. Place the tofu cubes on a lightly oiled baking sheet. Bake in the oven for 45 minutes until golden brown. Drizzle the tofu with 3 tablespoons of the reserved marinade and bake for another 5 minutes.

While the tofu bakes, prepare the steamed vegetables. Place the broccoli in a steamer basket over boiling water and cook for 4 minutes. Add the carrots and steam for 3 minutes. Add the water chestnuts and steam for 1 minute. Remove from the heat and spoon the vegetables onto a large serving platter. Place the tofu over the steamed vegetables, garnish with the green onion and serve immediately.

MAKES 4 SERVINGS.

Braised Tofu with Shiitake Mushrooms

The healthy ingredients in this dish combined with the flavor of the San-J Wakame Soup make this a winner!

Ingredients

1	package San-J Wakame Soup
8 ounces	boiling water
2 teaspoons	extra virgin olive oil
2	green onions, cut into 1-inch lengths
10	shiitake mushrooms, coarsely chopped
1 1/2 tablespoons	San-J Tamari
1 teaspoon	oyster sauce
1/2 teaspoon	sugar
12 ounces	extra-firm tofu, cut in 3/4-inch cubes
1 teaspoon	toasted sesame oil
4 cups	steamed white rice

In a small bowl, combine the San-J Wakame Soup and the boiling water, mixing until the dry soup is dissolved. Set aside. In a large wok or heavy skillet, heat the oil over high heat. Add the green onions and the mushrooms and stir-fry for 30 seconds. Add the dissolved San-J Wakame Soup, the San-J Tamari, the oyster sauce and the sugar. Stir to blend and bring to a boil. Add the tofu and let the mixture boil until it reduces by half, about 5 to 10 minutes. Stir in the sesame oil and serve immediately over the rice.

MAKES 4 SERVINGS.

Lean & Spicy Miso Turkey Burgers

San-J Schezuan Sauce and White Miso Soup infuse the ground turkey with intense, rich flavors.
It's a fun and delicious treat for the whole family.

Ingredients

1 pound	lean ground turkey
2	packages San-J White Miso Soup
2 teaspoons	San-J Schezuan Sauce
4	whole grain hamburger buns
4	romaine lettuce leaves, cleaned and chilled

In a medium bowl, combine the ground turkey, the dry San-J White Miso Soup mix and the San-J Schezuan Sauce. Mix well. Preheat an indoor or outdoor grill. Divide and shape the meat mixture into 4 patties. Grill the patties according to your preference, about 5 minutes on each side. Grill the whole grain hamburger buns to toast. Place the grilled burger on the hamburger bun and top each with a romaine lettuce leaf. Add any condiments of your choice.

MAKES 4 SERVINGS.

Green Leek & San-J Wakame Soup

The base for this good-for-you soup is San-J Wakame Soup.
Wakame is dried seaweed...a nutritional jolt for this tasty soup.

Ingredients

6 cups	water
4	packages San-J Wakame Soup
1 cup	leeks, thinly sliced
2 medium	carrots, thinly sliced
6 ounces	button mushrooms, sliced in half
1/2 cup	celery, thinly sliced
1/2 cup	frozen baby peas
3 tablespoons	dry sherry
2 tablespoons	San-J Tamari

In a large saucepan or Dutch oven, bring the water to a boil. Add the packages of the San-J Wakame Soup to the boiling water. Stir to dissolve and reduce the heat to low. Simmer for 5 minutes. Add the leeks, carrots, mushrooms and the celery. Stir and simmer for 5 minutes. Stir in the baby peas, the sherry and the San-J Tamari. Simmer for an additional 5 minutes and serve immediately.

MAKES 4 SERVINGS.

Glossary

BONITO – a type of tuna which is dried and shaved into flakes and used to add flavor to soups and sauces.

DASHI – soup stock made from dried fish flakes, kombu (seaweed) and water. It is a popular stock used in Japanese cooking.

EDAMAME – young whole soybeans that are cooked and eaten out of the pod. A great source of soy protein.

KOMBU – sometimes called kelp, kombu is seaweed which is used when making dashi (soup stock).

MIRIN – a sweet, golden wine made from glutinous rice. Essential to the Japanese cook, mirin adds sweetness and flavor to a variety of dishes, sauces and glazes. Mirin should be stored away from heat and light to preserve flavor.

MISO – fermented soybean paste. There are three basic types of miso — barley miso, rice miso and soybean miso. Miso's color, flavor and texture are affected by the amounts of soybeans, koji (mold) and salt used as well as the length of time it is aged, which can range from 6 months to 3 years. Miso is used in sauces, soups, marinades, dips, main dishes, salad dressings and as a table condiment. It's easily digested and extremely nutritious, having rich amounts of B vitamins and protein. Also called bean paste.

NORI – paper-thin sheets of dried seaweed. Its most common use is wrapping sushi, but can also be used as a seasoning or garnish when finely cut.

SAKE - a slightly sweet wine that is made from fermented rice. Sake is often used in Japanese cooking, particularly in sauces and marinades. Once opened, it will keep tightly sealed in the refrigerator for at least 3 weeks.

SASHIMI – slices or slabs of raw fish such as tuna or salmon. Usually served with thinly sliced ginger, finely shredded daikon radish and wasabi.

SHOYU – the Japanese word for "soy sauce." Shoyu is brewed with approximately equal portions of soybeans and wheat. Koji (mold) is added to the soybean /wheat mixture and fermented in salt water approximately 6 months. The Chinese word for soy sauce is "Soya."

SUSHI – although commonly thought to mean raw fish, sushi actually means rice flavored with a sweetened rice vinegar. The flavored rice is most commonly served with raw fish or rolled with fresh vegetables and is often wrapped with nori (seaweed).

SOBA - buckwheat noodles

SOMEN - white, threadlike wheat noodles

TAMARI – a premium soy sauce brewed with more soybeans than ordinary soy sauce for a smoother, richer, more complex taste. Tamari contains more soy protein than ordinary soy sauce giving it unique flavor-enhancing properties and superior stability when heated.

TOFU – made from curdled soymilk. Available in different varieties: silken, soft, firm and extra-firm. Silken can be substituted for cream cheese or sour cream. Firm can be crumbled or cubed and used as a meat substitute. Also known as soybean curd or bean curd.

UMAMI – considered the fifth taste receptor, in addition to sweet, sour, bitter and salty. Umami can be described as savory and deliciousness. The umami taste is triggered by glutamate which is an amino acid.

WAKAME – dark green seaweed can be found in dried or fresh forms. It is used like a vegetable by adding to soups and salads.

WASABI – commonly referred to as Asian horseradish, wasabi actually comes from the root of an Asian plant. It's used to make a green-colored condiment that has a sharp, pungent, fiery flavor.

Enjoy San-J's entire line of gourmet Asian products:

PREMIUM SOY SAUCE

Tamari Soy Sauce (also available in Reduced Sodium)

Organic Tamari Soy Sauce (also available in Reduced Sodium)

Organic Shoyu

COOKING/STIR-FRY SAUCES

Thai Peanut Sauce

Szechuan Sauce

Teriyaki Sauce

Sweet & Tangy Sauce

Asian BBQ Sauce

Japanese Steak Sauce

SOUPS

White Miso Soup Envelope

Wakame Soup Envelope

Mild Miso Soup Cup

Dark Miso Soup Cup

SALAD DRESSINGS

Tamari Sesame Dressing

Tamari Peanut Dressing

Tamari Vinaigrette Dressing

Tamari Mustard Dressing

GRILLING SAUCE

Cracked Pepper Sauce

Sweet & Hot Chili Sauce

RICE CRACKERS

Black Sesame Rice Crackers

Sesame Rice Crackers Tamari

Brown Rice Crackers

San-J products can be found at your local health food store
or grocery store. Visit our web site at **www.san-j.com**
for a link to order San-J products on-line.

Index